AF435925

With the support of the Comune di Siena - Department of Commerce, Tourism and Productive Activities

Viale Zara, 9 – 20159 Milano
tel. 02/87383764
www.enzimilab.com
info@enzimilab.com

www.morellinieditore.it
facebook.com/MorelliniEd/

Edited by Silvia Calvi
Translated by Christina Angelilli
Book cover and illustrations by Sara Rambaldi
Graphics by márGo

Photo credits: pages I, VIII, © Studio Fotografico Lensini - Copyright Opera della Metropolitana (Authorization n. 251/2023)

ISBN: 979-12-5527-060-7

First edition: 2019
Printed: Rotomail Italia S.p.A. – VIgnate (MI)

Lorenzo Bianciardi – Andrea Sguerri

Siena My Way

Illustrations by Sara Rambaldi
Translated by Christina Angelilli

MORELLINI EDITORE

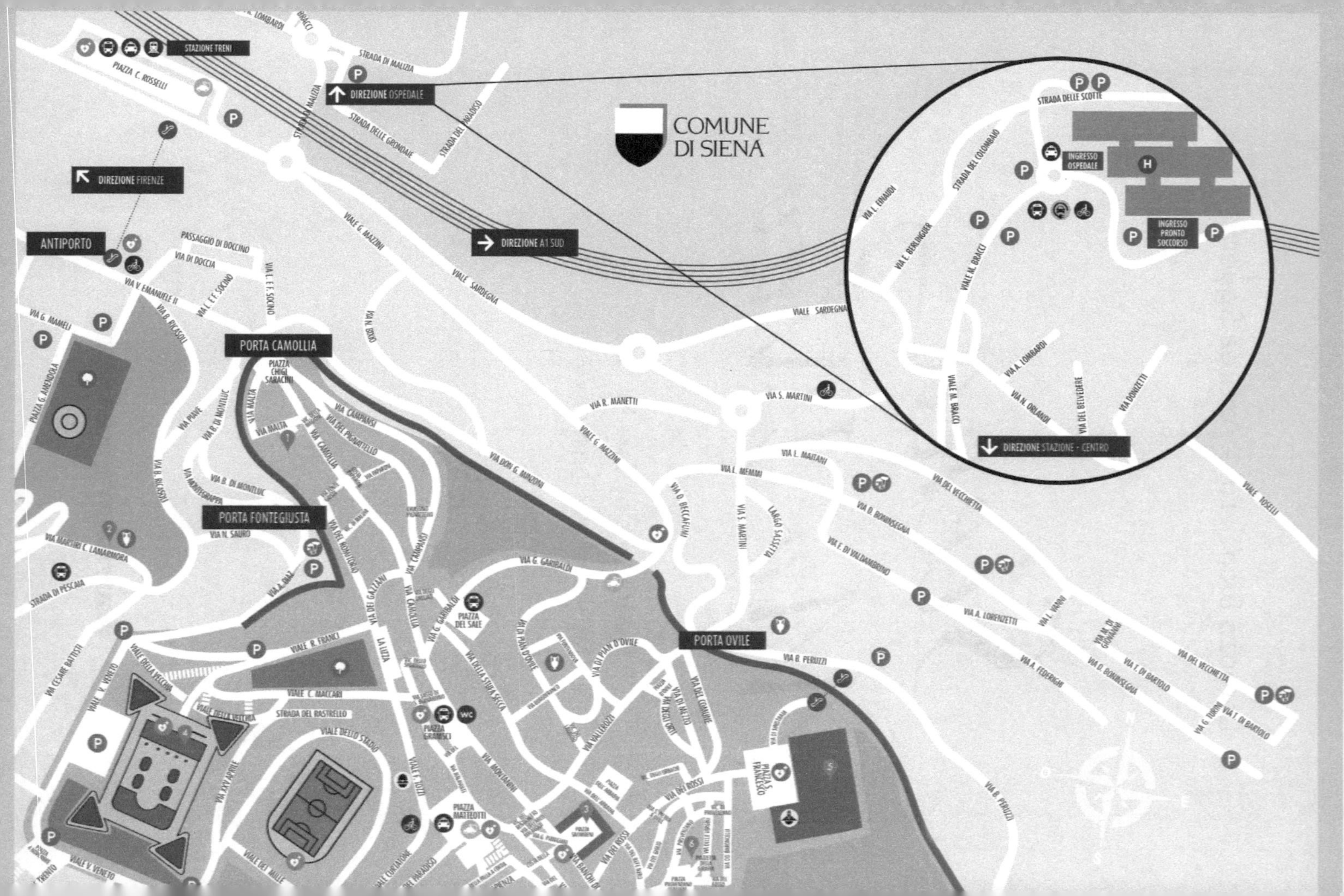

STAZIONE TRENI
PIAZZA C. ROSSELLI
DIREZIONE FIRENZE
ANTIPORTO
PASSAGGIO DI BOCCINO
VIA DI DOCCIA
VIA V. EMANUELE II
VIA L. E F. SOCINO
VIA G. MAMELI
VIA B. RICASOLI
VIALE G. MAZZINI
STRADA DI MALIZIA
STRADA DI MALIZIA
DIREZIONE OSPEDALE
STRADA DEL PARADISO
STRADA DELLE GRONDAIE
VIA LOMBARDI
BRACCI
COMUNE DI SIENA
DIREZIONE A1 SUD
VIALE SARDEGNA
VIALE SARDEGNA
VIA N. BIXIO
STRADA DELLE SCOTTE
STRADA DEL COLOMBAIO
INGRESSO OSPEDALE
H
INGRESSO PRONTO SOCCORSO
VIA L. EINAUDI
VIA E. BERLINGUER
VIALE M. BRACCI
VIALE M. BRACCI
VIA A. LOMBARDI
VIA N. ORLANDI
VIA DEL BELVEDERE
VIA DONIZETTI
VIALE TOSELLI
DIREZIONE STAZIONE - CENTRO
PORTA CAMOLLIA
PIAZZA CHIGI SARACINI
PIAZZA G. AMENDOLA
VIA R. DI MONTLUC
VIA MALTA
VIA MALTA
VIA PIAVE
VIA CAMPANSI
VIA DEL PIGNATTELLO
VIA B. DI MONTLUC
VIA MONTEGRAPPA
PORTA FONTEGIUSTA
VIA N. SAURO
VIA A. DIAZ
VIA MARTIRI C. LAMARMORA
STRADA DI PESCAIA
VIA CAMOLLIA
VIA DON G. MINZONI
VIA R. MANETTI
VIALE G. MAZZINI
VIA S. MARTINI
VIA O. BECCAFUMI
VIA L. MEMMI
VIA S. MARTINI
LARGO SASSETTA
VIA E. MAITANI
VIA DEL VECCHIETTA
VIA B. BUONISEGNA
VIA F. DI VALDAMBRINO
VIA A. LORENZETTI
VIA L. VANNI
VIA M. DI GIOVANNI
VIA A. FEDERIGHI
VIA O. BUONISEGNA
VIA T. DI BARTOLO
VIA DEL VECCHIETTA
VIA G. TORRINI
VIA T. DI BARTOLO
VIA B. PERUZZI
VIA B. PERUZZI
VIA G. GARIBALDI
VIA G. GARIBALDI
VIA DEI GAZZANI
LA LIZZA
VIALE R. FRANCI
PIAZZA DEL SALE
VIA DI PIAN D'OVILE
VIA DI PIAN D'OVILE
VIA DELLA STUFA SECCA
PORTA OVILE
VIA DEL COMUNE
VIA DI MEZZO
VIA DEGLI ORTI
PIAZZA S. FRANCESCO
VIA CESARE BATTISTI
VIALE R. VENETO
VIALE DELLA VECCHIA
VIALE C. MACCARI
STRADA DEL RASTRELLO
VIALE DELLO STADIO
PIAZZA GRAMSCI
WC
VIA XXV APRILE
VIALE F. TOZZI
VIA MONTANINI
PIAZZA MATTEOTTI
VIA DEI ROSSI
VIALE DEI MILLE
VIALE V. VENETO
PRATO

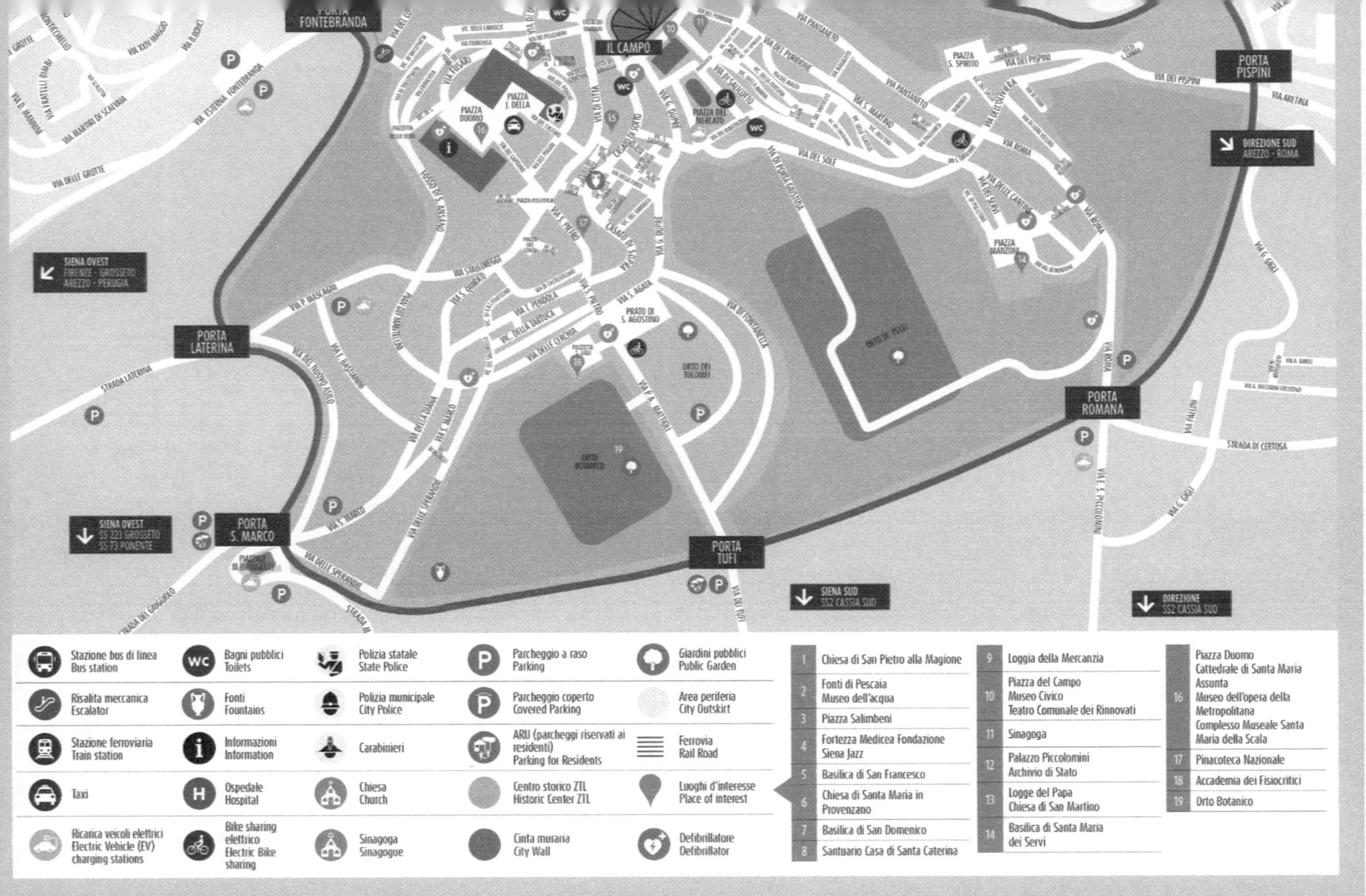

PORTA FONTEBRANDA
IL CAMPO
PORTA PISPINI
PIAZZA S. SPIRITO
VIA DEI PISPINI
VIA DEI PISPINI
VIA ARETINA
DIREZIONE SUD
AREZZO - ROMA
VIA PANTANETO
PIAZZA J. DELLA
PIAZZA DUOMO
PIAZZA DEL MERCATO
VIA DI CITTÀ
VIA G. DUPRE
VIA S. MARTINO
VIA ROMA
VIA DELLE CANTINE
VIA DEI SERVI
VIA ROMA
VIA DEL SOLE
VIA DI PORTA GIUSTIZA
PIAZZA MANZONI
SIENA OVEST
FIRENZE - GROSSETO
AREZZO - PERUGIA
ROSSO DI S. ANSANO
CASATO DI SOTTO
CASATO DI SOPRA
VIA S. PIETRO
VIA S. PIETRO
VIA S. AGATA
PRATO DI S. AGOSTINO
VIA DI FONTANELLA
ORTO DEI PELLI
PORTA LATERINA
VIA DEL NUOVO ASILO
VIA S. MARCO
VIA P. MASCAGNI
VIA E. PENDOLA
VIC. DELLA TARTUCA
VIA DELLE CERCHIA
VIA DELLA DIANA
VIA P. A. MATTIOLI
ORTO DEI TOLOMEI
STRADA LATERINA
PORTA ROMANA
VIA ROMA
VIA PALLINI
STRADA DI CERTOSA
VIA G. GIGLI
VIA E. S. PICCOLOMINI
SIENA OVEST
SS 223 GROSSETO
SS 73 PONENTE
PORTA S. MARCO
VIA DELLE SPERANDIE
PORTA TUFI
VIA DEI TUFI
ORTO BOTANICO
SIENA SUD
SS2 CASSIA SUD
DIREZIONE
SS2 CASSIA SUD

Stazione bus di linea — Bus station
Risalita meccanica — Escalator
Stazione ferroviaria — Train station
Taxi
Ricarica veicoli elettrici Electric Vehicle (EV) charging stations
Bagni pubblici — Toilets
Fonti — Fountains
Informazioni — Information
Ospedale — Hospital
Bike sharing elettrico Electric Bike sharing
Polizia statale — State Police
Polizia municipale — City Police
Carabinieri
Chiesa — Church
Sinagoga — Synagogue
Parcheggio a raso — Parking
Parcheggio coperto — Covered Parking
ARU (parcheggi riservati ai residenti) Parking for Residents
Centro storico ZTL — Historic Center ZTL
Cinta muraria — City Wall
Giardini pubblici — Public Garden
Area periferia — City Outskirt
Ferrovia — Rail Road
Luoghi d'interesse — Place of interest
Defibrillatore — Defibrillator
1 Chiesa di San Pietro alla Magione
2 Fonti di Pescaia Museo dell'acqua
3 Piazza Salimbeni
4 Fortezza Medicea Fondazione Siena Jazz
5 Basilica di San Francesco
6 Chiesa di Santa Maria in Provenzano
7 Basilica di San Domenico
8 Santuario Casa di Santa Caterina
9 Loggia della Mercanzia
10 Piazza del Campo Museo Civico Teatro Comunale dei Rinnovati
11 Sinagoga
12 Palazzo Piccolomini Archivio di Stato
13 Logge del Papa Chiesa di San Martino
14 Basilica di Santa Maria dei Servi
Piazza Duomo Cattedrale di Santa Maria Assunta
16 Museo dell'opera della Metropolitana Complesso Museale Santa Maria della Scala
17 Pinacoteca Nazionale
18 Accademia dei Fisiocritici
19 Orto Botanico

Index

Preface / 10 Travelers

Itineraries to Discover Siena and Live Like a Local

At a certain point we had had enough of big cities. Not at all because of the chaos, the noise or the temptations, but mostly because we were tired of the repetitiveness. We know, it seems like a contradiction, since every capital has its history, its quirks, its colors. Still, for world travelers like us, all the images of the many places our eyes have explored and the many flavors we've savored have all jumbled together in our minds. On the other hand, in an attempt to satisfy the majority of tastes, so many standard places and spaces have been created that, at a certain point, you seem more like the protagonist of *Groundhog Day*, than a tourist looking for a pleasant evening. This is why we are fed up.

The time to veer towards a more temperate dock had come. A destination that could help quiet the unsure sea of our thoughts. In order to find the right port, we did something we had always dreamed of: eyes closed, globe in our hands, index finger pointed towards the unknown, ready to stop the rotation of this miniature world. Stop. We open our eyes: Italy. Well, it could have gone worse. Thinking of Rome and Naples as a tranquil port makes us laugh. We need a smaller city that knows how to accommodate us.

Open Google Maps: zoom in four times on the boot, Tuscany comes into view. Siena is the first name that appears. Siena, we like the sound. Fine food and wines flash before our eyes; and then that crazy, colorful horse race we aren't sure we understand, but has always come to our attention. Sure, it's a lot, but it can't be everything. Further because, if that were it, we wouldn't have much motivation to get there, and yet, as we look at the computer screen, we're already mentally making a list of what to pack. We won't need much; we can get the essentials on-site. Yes, because smiles, looks, words and song are all difficult things to box up. They must be relished *in loco*.

Ok, we're ready. Depart, arrive, discover, encounter. Time to get our thoughts together and the will to put pen to paper, to capture, like a slightly faded Polaroid, the streets, places, emotions alive in a city that preserves a tremendous amount of magic that, to the observant eye, is visible in every corner and every alleyway.

This is what we came here for: to tell you something more about this city, how any traveler like us can live it.

Chapter 1 / The Eternal Child

Wonder in his Eyes

The first surprises while flying over the city

All children, except for one, eventually grow up. That one is me. I realized early on when I noticed my friends start to change, not only physically, but in their way of thinking: they learned new rules, they became more and more serious, more conscientious, and they got used to the world around them.

It wasn't like that for me. When coming into contact with new things, there has always been a look of wonder on my face: I give myself up to curiosity, without paying attention to the time that passes. In those moments I've never felt uncomfortable, but rather on a continuous discovery of secrets, of new elements surrounding me, breathing in the essence of the most invisible things.

I haven't changed much since then. I continue to look at the world through the eyes of a child. Even though I've learned to do new, more complex things, such as flying. What's to it? You just need to get high enough, look ahead, close your eyes and wait to lift off from the ground. Your imagination does the rest. There's just one condition, and that's the hardest part: you have to give your imagination total power to create what your heart suggests. Amaze, imagine, compose. Easy, no?

When I first arrived here, I immediately looked for the right place to takeoff, above the rooftops and the cupolas. The **Fortezza Medicea** (**fortress**) seemed the ideal spot, with that breathtaking view of one of the most poetic profiles of the city.

Siena is so beautiful from above, with its sinuous shape that adheres to the terrain's natural slopes. I follow the walls of the city so that I can embrace it with my eyes: the **Torre del Mangia** and **Piazza del Campo** will be an ideal landing spot, but first I want to soak up the elegance of the spires of the **Duomo**, the massive presence of the basilicas of **San Francesco** and **San Domenico**, the intrigue of the alleys and streets marking the city like the lines on a wise, elderly woman. I slowly begin my descent with open arms and my gaze on the shining white facade of **Santa Maria in Provenzano**. From above it's even more peculiar to see how the countryside weaves its way in and out of the city center, in a triumph of green that contrasts with the color of the brick towers and buildings.

It's time to land, but it doesn't necessarily mean "keeping my feet on the ground." In fact, as my shoes hit the center of the piazza, in the shadow of the Torre del Mangia, I can feel that classic expression on my face. How can one not be completely amazed when confronted with such beauty? I don't know how long I've been looking up when I feel someone graze my shoulder. Standing behind me is a man with a strange fire-red hat, dressed in medieval garb, gesturing and inviting me to follow him.

Who knows, maybe that's just what they do around here, and seeing that I don't know anything about this city, I don't see why I shouldn't accept. Maybe he'll satisfy my curiosity, and as we are still here, I want to ask him about why this magnificent, shell-shaped *piazza* is divided into **nine sections**. I decide to work up enough courage and I ask him. At first he looks at me a bit strange, but then he gazes towards the sky and, with a clear and content voice says: "the history of this piazza is long and complex; at the beginning it was just a large field that collected rain water. Most activity within the city was higher up, in the **Castelvecchio** district. As years passed, with the first governments of the Republic of Siena, the space began to be used for fairs, games and markets. The **Government of**

the Nine, in the beginning of the 14th century, idealized both the **Palazzo Pubblico** in front of you, and the paving of the piazza, with its characteristic **bricks** laid out in a fish bone pattern. The nine slices are, in fact, in honor of those forward-thinking governors."

And the tower? "It represents the symbol of civil power, and if you look closely enough, its merlons reach the same height as the steeple of the Duomo, symbol of religious power, even though it's located higher up. Personally, I am allergic to every form of power, but the concept of equality is quite interesting to me: the spirit of Siena can be found right here. They had to reach 102 meters to get there, but the result is commendable."

I suddenly realize that I don't even know the name of my companion; before I have the chance to ask, he introduces himself as Francesco Angiolieri[1], **Cecco** for short, local poet. His name is familiar, and as I stand there contemplating, he has already started to talk again. "If you want to climb to the top, go right ahead. There are almost 400 steps but it's worth it. If you would rather know why the Torre del Mangia (tower of the Eater) has this particular name, buy me something to drink and I'll tell you all about it." In front of a glass

---

1   Francesco Angiolieri: Sienese poet (circa 1260 – 1311), known for his comedic style and infamous for his predilection of drinking and gambling. (https://www.treccani.it/enciclopedia/cecco-angiolieri/).

of red wine, he recounts how the first bell ringer commissioned by the Sienese Government to sound the hours was a certain Giovanni di Balduccio, famous in Siena for his innate capacity to squander his money. The Sienese, capable of giving nicknames even to a stone, didn't waste time in baptizing him **Mangiaguadagni (the Eater of Earnings)**, or simply Mangia (the Eater). Since that time the tower's name has remained the same.

Over a second glass he tells me that Siena, with its irregular shape made up of alleyways and hills, is divided into three **Terzi (Thirds)**, rather three areas within the medieval walls: the Terzo di Città, the Terzo di Camollia (with the accent on the i) and the Terzo di San Martino. I start to wonder about something so I interrupt him: and what about the *contrade*[2]? With an unconcerned smile he responds: "Of course, the contrade are within the Thirds. The *Terzo di Città* was the first to expand both in number of inhabitants and buildings, but with the growing number of pilgrims passing along the **Via Francigena** (the road that, even before the 11th century, united North and South Europe, from Canterbury to Rome, leading all the way to the ports of Puglia), *San Martino* and *Camollia* quickly prospered. As population grew, so did the perimeter of the city, thus in order to protect it they constructed high and wide **walls** and **gates**, that remained open to welcome merchants and visitors, but could also be tightly closed to ward off enemy assaults; go to see them if you have time, some are still intact."

Another majestic tower sticks out from the spot where we are comfortably seated, that of the cathedral, on top of the hill, not in brick but black and white marble, or at least that's what it seems from afar. "Remember the colors of the **Balzana**, the crest of Siena, whose medieval origins conceal a legend tied to the founding of the city by Senio and Aschio, the legendary twin sons of Remus, who escaped from their perfidious uncle Romulus? Not knowing how to elude

---

2   *Contrada* is the word that refers to the division of Siena's historical center in 17 districts or neighborhoods. Plural: *contrade.*

him, the twins asked for help from the gods, who sent two horses, one white, one black, that assisted the twins in reaching these hills. Here they marked the first perimeters of the future Siena, adapting Senio's name. Reacting to the confused expression on my face, he continues: "My boy, you don't seem too knowledgeable in history and literature, am I right? Here in Siena there is an exceptional **University**, that even in my time was hosting the most brilliant minds in Europe. It was founded in 1240 and since then has never ceased welcoming students into its classrooms from every corner of the continent, so much so that it has left our city with a remarkable cultural legacy. The university's first courses were Law and Medicine, but now there are many others: you should stop and visit one of these days."

We finish a third glass and pay as we leave to go take a walk. I'm not ready to leave my guide, so I continue to assail him with questions: and that marble chapel next to the *Palazzo Pubblico*? And that fountain over there? "Slow down, son, one thing at a time. The **Chapel** is the only building that juts out into the piazza, constructed in the second half of the 14th century in honor of the Virgin Mary for saving many from a historical disaster: the famous **Black Death**. Now, the fountain that you mentioned goes back to just a few years before; its inauguration represented something of a miracle for the Sienese. You must know that, if there's one thing Siena doesn't have, it's water. This has always been one of Siena's biggest dilemmas: where to find it and how to get it up here. If only the mythological underground river of pure water, the **Diana**, truly existed, life in Siena would have surely been different. What a shame that it was never found and remains to this day a legend."

He continues: "There is some water nearby, and it was brought to the city by underground channels that you can still see today, the so-called **bottini**. Going back to the fountain, it was such a joy for the people of Siena to see water flow in Piazza del Campo that they immediately named it the **Fonte Gaia (fountain of joy)**. What you see today is a commendable reproduction sculpted in the 19th century by Tito Sarrocchi, while the original marble sculptures by the brilliant Jacopo della Quercia can be admired within the **Santa Maria della Scala Museum**. There are fountains in every corner of the city, still filled with this "gracious" water. These many fountains have acted as social centers and meeting points for centuries; some, such as the one nestled in the **Valle di Follonica**, have been recently restored to their original grandeur."

As Cecco speaks we exit the *piazza* from the **Costa dei Barbieri** (better known to the Sienese as **Costarella**). I'm not sure where he's taking me, but I feel that with each step I'm more and more curious about truly understanding this small-big city. At the top of the hill, in front of us, there is a stone tower. There are many, but I notice something strange about them: they are all different heights. "You're right. The tower, in the Middle Ages and afterwards, was a symbol of power, a visual reminder to those passing just how important the family was who erected it. However, if Lady Fortune, with her eternally spinning wheel, were to turn away from those once powerful, those taking their place would be sure to make noticeable changes. The tower, and what it represents, would immediately be partially destroyed, and then rebuilt according to the new family's role."

He speaks as fast as he walks, this Cecco, and I remain a bit behind not only on the street, but also amongst my growing list of things to ask him, crowded in the confusion in my head. One thing I forgot to mention, though, has to do with the symbols and colors strewn around the city. They are like strange, colorful **crests** hanging on street corners, as if marking a territory. "**Exactly** right. What you see are the exact points marking the borders of the *contrade* running in the **Palio**, a true tradition in Siena, where history, passion and magic combine better than the colors of an expert painter's palette. Today there are 17, but it hasn't always been this way. Some, in the past, were incorporated into others and thus suppressed." We continue our walk up the street Cecco tells me is called **Via di Città**: among the adorned buildings several balconies and courtyards stand out, as the rhythm of daily life continues.

At a certain point we turn right, onto a small street that climbs a bit higher than others we've passed and leads onto a hill where an architectural miracle lays, the **Duomo** of Siena. On our way there, we pass under an enormous arch, or maybe a gate, I'm not sure. The strange thing is that it doesn't seem to lead to anything, just delineates a side of the *piazza*.

"This is the illustrious **Facciatone**. You must know that the Sienese have always been very ambitious. After having built the cathedral, one of the largest in all of Christianity, they realized they weren't satisfied and idealized a project that was equal parts genius and madness. The body of the actual church would become the transect of a colossal cathedral that would have encompassed, with its nave, the entire area where we are walking now. What you earlier called an arch, would have been none other than the facade of the 'new Duomo,' unfathomable dimensions not only for the Middle Ages, but even your time. The arrival of the Black Plague and the realization that the sheer weight of all those stones and bricks would have buckled the hill that had already began to 'slide' downwards, brought the feet of the engineers back to the ground. But by then the *Facciatone*, as you can see it, had already been built, and equipped with an internal staircase going all the way to the walkway at the top. If the stairs of the Torre del Mangia weren't enough for you, try these: I can assure you that the view is breathtaking."

I didn't have the heart to tell him that I came here flying, already having enjoyed the beauty of this city from above; mostly because I don't want to contradict him too much, but also because, as I'm thinking about the best way to tell him, he is already up the stairs, towards the main entrance. As I try to reach him, I am literally bombarded by a myriad of sculptures characterizing the facade. Not only prophets, patriarchs, and philosophers, but also mysterious creatures and **gargoyles**, with their mouths wide open towards the gothic spires.

Now he's pulling me along by my jacket, he doesn't want me to linger too much. In fact, I am following him again, down the steep stairs leading to the **Battistero (Baptistery)**. Particularly steep. I realize this as my rear-end violently hits a step. "Did you slip? Don't worry, you're not alone. Do you see that **cross** in black marble there, right next to you, carved into the step? If you ask around they will tell you that **St. Catherine**, on her way to the Santa Maria della Scala Hospital to help with the poor, 'pushed' by the devil, fell right in that spot." I felt more comforted by the view of the *Battistero* and the **Piazza San Giovanni**, one of Siena's many treasures, than by Cecco's words.

Tourists bump into us, but no one seems to really see us. My guide has begun to talk again, or rather mumble about how times have changed. "If I were running Siena, things would be going much better, I can guarantee…" Yes, I can imagine. *Osterie* open 24/7. I realize that my thoughts were not silent, but instead spoken out loud. "Good job, I can see that you're not lacking in irony, this is the spirit that we appreciate in Siena. But if you truly want to understand this city, don't just walk around distractedly. Take your time, go into the museums, courtyards, secret nooks. Search out a place that is just yours, abandon yourself to wonder and reflection. Only if you allow your mind to wander can it find rest, be restored and become creative. Maybe you won't learn to write poetry as well as I do, but something will come out of it." I'm not sure why, but I don't doubt it.

As we continue to walk, streets and alleyways pass in front of my eyes; after a few sharp turns we find ourselves in front of the small tunnel that leads to a courtyard named the **Castellare degli Ugurgeri** marked by a stone sign. It seems like Cecco moves around these areas with a certain familiarity. Leaving, he leads me to back to the street, where he points to another sign that indicates that this building was built by his grandfather. Just as I'm about to ask him for an explanation, I realize I don't hear his voice anymore. I turn around. He's gone. I try looking for him through a doorway, but in vain; a passerby asks if I need help, but something in me suggests I better not tell him that I'm looking for a certain Cecco Angiolieri, local poet.

I begin to think that maybe the time has come for me to roll up my sleeves and begin to go out on my own, visiting the city in an ordinary way, as do most tourists, buying a guidebook and following its standard itineraries. Or maybe not. Oh, there is something I haven't told you. I've perfected another talent, that of knowing how to look at things through the eyes of others, so much so that I become them.

This is what I want to do: see this city with many different eyes, many different spirits, so that I can be a romantic, an athlete, a foodie, an explorer. In short, so that I can say I saw and lived the different sides of this city. As I carry on, looking for these sides of myself, a few verses of a poem by Pessoa come to mind:

> *I'm capable of feeling the same wonder*
> *A newborn child would feel*
> *If he noticed that he'd really and truly been born*
> *I feel at each moment that I'd just been born*
> *Into a completely new world...*[3]

---

3   © Translation: 2006, Richard Zenith.
From: A Little Larger Than the Entire Universe: Selected Poems
Publisher: Penguin, New York, 2006.
(https://www.poetryinternational.com/en/poets-poems/poems/poem/103-7052_THE-KEEPER-OF-SHEEP-II).

Head in the Clouds

Losing yourself in Siena like a perpetual dreamer

How beautiful is a sleeping Siena in the early hours in the morning, how many empty streets. Strolling in the deserted city inundates me with positive energy: dim lights begin to show over the horizon and the first warm rays of the sun, so pale, wake up my body little by little. I still get goosebumps thinking about my first trip to Siena. I was young, a carefree 18-year-old on her first trip out of town: what a wonderful welcome this magical place had reserved for me, how many emotions…

Flashback: I relive my first "encounters" with the Duomo and, in particular, Piazza del Campo, at sunrise, with those orange rays of sun that I wish hadn't let in the vivid yellow of the day; it was a sweet and sensual awakening, with the first aromas of the of city, that smell of tepid sandstone; the touch of those medieval walls, still humid from the night before, with some tufts of grass poking out here and there among the bricks combined with the most pleasant and reassuring travel companion: the sound of the church bells at every hour that never leaves me.

If I close and reopen my eyes, I see myself lost in these streets that don't really lead to anywhere, maybe just to a state of mind, that is truly the only thing I look for when I explore a new city. A sensation that reaches my heart before my mind, something to treasure within me.

Exploring the **Fosso di Sant'Ansano** by foot and entering the solitary **Vicolo delle Carrozze** is like taking an imaginary leap into another era. I can imagine the 17th century noblemen, with their cloaks and big boots, getting out of their carriages and tying their horses along this narrow street. Stopping at the "Ostaria della Scala" tavern, they accompany their ladies, chilly in their ermine hand muffs and wrapped up in the soft velvet brocade of their elegant clothing.

We are on the **"ponte" di Diacceto** ("bridge" about halfway down via Diacceto); gazing up towards the cathedral's bell tower, we find ourselves in front of the facade of an impressive building, on which, mounted in a long red rectangle between two rows of windows is the sign "Albergo e Ristoratore La Scala", La Scala Restaurant and Hotel. Reading this slightly discolored sign, exactly where it has been for hundreds of years, reassures me: proof that not all past fades with modernity.

On the days of the Palio, you might get lucky enough to see horses being led down this alley, just as they did centuries ago: it's the *Selva contrada* that gets to honor its origins in this narrow, dark alley, transforming it into the stable where the race's protagonist is housed.

This is Siena: you find traces of the past at every corner. From **Via di Diacceto** (*diaccio* is Tuscan for the Italian term for ice, *ghiaccio*, and this is where they historically stored the snow gathered from the winter in holes dug in the rock), in just a few steps you reach the adjacent **Via della Galluzza**, that descends into the Fontebranda neighborhood. From here, passing under a noble 15th century *trifora* (three-part window), your gaze lands on eight arches that seem to frame the street in a lace pattern. I've read and studied a bit, because here the atmosphere is truly intriguing: the arches are 19th century and not decorative but were added to support the precarious buildings damaged in the 1798 earthquake. And what's the story behind the name of this street?

Via della Galluzza, like its neighboring **Via di Beccheria**, was known for the poultry market; but the etymology of the word brings to mind *galla* or *gallozza*, an ancient way of creating ink and colors from a liquid that forms inside a hole dug in tree bark by a particular insect. It's not a surprise, then, that this district was known in medieval times for the "art of wool," where they tanned leather and dyed wool. **Vicolo della Macina, Vicolo del Tiratoio** transport me back in time, to that kaleidoscope of colors, from emerald green to yellow ochre, like a painter's palette, while in the background the deafening and continuous noise of the fulling mills from once upon a time. And breathing in that smell, not always so pleasant, coming from the skins and clothing hung to dry in the streets.

Surely there was no lack of water at this intersection, as we are so close to the famous **Fontebranda** fountain. Even Dante mentions it on a marble gravestone in the falsifiers pit in his Inferno "But could I see the miserable souls/Of Guido, Alessandro, or their brother,/I'd not give up the sight for *Fonte Branda*.[1]" With is merlons and three gothic arches, the fountain was the most beautiful one in the city, so much so that the condemned figure who pronounces this sentence, the Florentine counterfeiter Mastro Adamo would have happily given up the chance to place his eyes on the waters of this fountain so that certain despised acquaintances of his would be condemned along with him.

I take a minute to rest in the warmth of the sun, listening to the gurgle of the fountain that reminds me of an old music box, before tackling the hill that from **Via Santa Caterina** passes along to **Via dei Pittori**, bordering the **Casa Santuario di Santa Caterina (House of St. Catherine)**. Known as the portico "of the cities of Italy," it opens to a view with those lean columns which support an atrium attributed to Baldassarre Peruzzi. After admiring the travertine well in the right corner of the courtyard, I pass through the door of the complex to reach a second atrium that connects the **Chiesa del Crocifisso** (on the right) to the **Oratorio della Cucina** (on the left).

According to tradition, these areas became the kitchen of Saint Catherine's family in her original home. It's exciting to walk through the oratory and enter the "heart" of the saint's home: the checkered, wooden ceiling, gold on blue, is enchanting, I admire the different scenes paint-

---

1   Dante Alighieri, *The Divine Comedy*, Inferno XXX, 76-78. Translated from the original *"Ma s'io vedessi qui l'anima trista di Guido o d'Alessandro o di lor frate, per Fonte Branda non darei la vista"* (https://digitaldante.columbia.edu/dante/divine-comedy/inferno/inferno-30/)

ed on the walls that recount important moments of St. Catherine's life. I discover more as I lower my gaze: 16th century Renaissance ceramic floor tiles. It is here that I notice a man who has sat himself aside in silent meditation and I think he must be particularly religious.

I stop to reflect, thinking about the ancient home of the Benincasa family, and let my mind wander. As the sun's rays grow stronger, I find shelter in the shade provided by the majestic **Basilica di San Domenico**, but before I get there something else catches my attention, a space between two buildings: **Vicolo della Pallacorda** (meaning rope-ball). I'm not an athlete but thinking about a tennis match in medieval times makes me smile; I imagine that here they probably played catch over a cord hanging in the middle of the street, centuries before the wooden racket covered in parchment was introduced.

These walls have seen their fill of games since the late Middle Ages! My dream would be to come back here as a child to experience playing hide and seek, statues or blind man's bluff with my friends. How many stories could these romantic arches framing the street tell us! Long and narrow, Vicolo della Pallacorda seems closed-off, as if protecting the children from the *Drago Contrada* who play here all year long, or even the Palio horse in its stable here in the Camporegio district.

Camporegio is the name of one of the streets that first enchanted me, where I got lost in Siena's splendor; the Basilica di San Domenico, the cathedral, the rooftops of the city and the Torre del Mangia have all captivated me. Seeing Siena from here seems almost like a nativity scene, wrapped in warm light. The perfect place for dreaming. Before ducking into **Vicolo del Campaccio** I close my eyes for just a moment, trying to forever capture all this beauty in my memory.

In moments like this, the only thing that truly satisfies my imagination is a good, dusty book. Just a few steps away is **Via della Sapienza**: I'm sure I will be able to discover something new at the **Biblioteca comunale degli Intronati**, Siena's public library. Once inside, passing through the "historical room" of antique volumes and manuscripts, or in the "Gabinetto drawings and prints" on the first floor, is like opening a treasure chest! You are sure to find a precious gem among the 10.000 drawings or 28.000 prints. If you are crazy for historical postcards, publicity fliers or even photograph rolls like me, you can pass hours and hours with these in a separate collection. A bit like going through an old trunk in the attic.

If browsing around here hasn't satisfied your hunger for books, I recommend checking out the narrow halls of the **Biblioteca Umanistica**, the Humanities Library. Walking in from the courtyard of the **Palazzo San Galgano** in **Via Roma**, after speaking with the doormen in Via di Fieravecchia, I discovered that it dates back to the founding of the University of Siena's Department of Letters and Philosophy in the 1970's. Who knows how many illustrious professors touched the same volumes. The basement seems part of another world, where I can lose myself in psychology and foreign literature, browse journals and "travel" among art, theater, music and cinema. The "reading room" on the ground floor is a delightful spot, silent and perfect for studying, with direct access to an enchanting small garden where you can sit and enjoy some sun.

The right book to comfort you is there, waiting. I found mine among Charles Dickens' travel diaries: it's called *Pictures from Italy* (1846) and contains passages from his stay in Tuscany. It's so exciting to find Siena described as a "piece of Venice, without the water." I do prefer buying certain books so I can keep them with me always; if this is the case, apart from larger bookstore chains such as Feltrinelli and Mondadori, there are three local bookstores worth a glance. The **Libreria Senese**, in the central Via di Città since 1974 (www.libreriasenese.it); outside of the historical center complete with café, is the modern **Becarelli** (www.labecarelli.it); and the most recent **Rebecca** in Via Pantaneto (rebeccalibreria@gmail.com), an independent female-run bookstore housing additional spaces dedicated to music and cinema.

Reading awakens the romantic in me: the 17 *contrada* **fountains** come to mind. Just think of how many "kisses" they've received by Sienese and tourists alike that have pursed their thirsty lips to take a drink! With their strange shapes, resembling mythological animals, and water that gushes out and baptizes its newest members. I would walk up and down all of Siena just to touch all seventeen of them again.

I still get goosebumps when I walk past the *Bruco Contrada's* fountain, at the end of **Via dei Rossi**, just before going down Via del Comune. I sit on the stone bench in front of the 15th century Fonte di San Francesco, under the arch that bears the weight of the street above (at the irons of St. Francis, some may say, right under that beautiful wrought iron railing), listening to the water babbling as if in a sort of cave. As I look toward the street, a new surprise thrills me: the statue of a seminude woman with long hair in the window. She observes me, opening the curtains from above, framed by bricks.

At number 123 in Via dei Rossi, these *Facing Windows* - as I like to call them after Ozpetek's dreamy film - attract all the attention. Try to observe the details. The white Carrara marble, the delicate gesture of the hand that pushes aside the sandstone curtains; the bronze pomegranate, symbol of fertility and life, crowned by a caterpillar (an *homage* to the *contrada*). I linger a bit to daydream about this heart-felt gift by the sculptor Pier Luigi Olla, entitled *Donna alla finestra* (*Woman at the window* - 1995): who knows why this elegant lady has such a sad air about her. I still wonder who she's expecting.

There are endless curiosities in this neighborhood: I pass under the arch of **Vicolo degli Orbachi** and I enter this tortuous street. Legend has it that this street was once one of the most infamous alleys in all of Siena, so dark that it was also called **Chiasso Buio (dark alley)**. Fortunately, today there's nothing to be afraid of. Instead, I suggest you venture under that arch on the left, because the world that it opens up to you will not disappoint: you are entering, in fact, what was once called **Via degli Orbachi di dentro**, a medieval street that used to run into Via dell'Abbadia and is now a dead end. A street romantically paved in brick and, squeezed among the buildings, two "fake" balconies called sporti (but if you want to know more about these, ask The Explorer).

I take my time heading back so I can take in the view of the rooftops and Orbachi gardens, of the vivid, steep buildings on **Via del Comune**, amassed one on top of the other. Salmon pink, cream, sand, yellow, ochre: my eyes reflect the pastel colors of the houses that climb the hill and nestle into the original city walls from the thirteenth century (therein the name of the street).

All of a sudden I realize that I've gotten myself lost again, because I was following the aroma of bay leaf as it invaded my senses, and my thoughts are up in the clouds with the birds. Bay trees grew abundantly in this green valley; and the *orbacca*, bay tree berry, is the fruit of the tree that this street was named after. So much beauty! This is the perfect place for lovers, where I can still remember my first kiss. An eternal, unforgettable kiss.

I come back to earth, open my eyes and continue to wander around **Via dei Baroncelli** and the parallel **Via delle Vergini**, two steep streets that lead you down into the *Giraffa Contrada*, at the intersection of **Vicolo della Viola**. This area doesn't seem to be very industriuos; if what Manzoni in *The Betrothed* says is true, then the "barons" in medieval times were not only nobles but also "derelicts." Turning our thoughts to the "virgins" recalled in this street's name, one mustn't think of nuns, but of the prostitutes that populated this district during the mid-16th century Spanish dominion. "Viola" may have been the name of a particularly famous courtesan in Siena and, in fact, up until the 1700's the street was called "Vicolo del Buon Costume," alley of good manners, for good reason.

So much history is hidden in the streets of Siena! Another anecdote I love brings me to **Via Pagliaresi**, better known to the Sienese as **Cane e Gatto**, dog and cat. Interesting name, isn't it? Legend has it that two rival families lived here, the Anigoleschi (or Arrigoleschi) and the Pelacani, who were always fighting on the street, just like cats and dogs. My intellectual friend might turn up her nose or would prefer to clarify that the place name actually comes from the family's nicknames, Anigoleschi becoming *gatto* (cat), and Pelacani becoming *cane* (dog). Feel free to choose which story to believe - I prefer the most imaginative one, as I laugh while thinking about two important families quarreling like two house pets.

I didn't come all the way over here just for this. Halfway down Cane e Gatto, my "street of wonders," **Vicolo degli Orefici**, begins its windy way. One of my favorite streets, a long secret passage for hiding away from the world, where I can find shelter for my thoughts away from the chaos that surrounds them. Passing under a dark arch, not knowing where it ends, I soon am enchanted by its silence and the view of arches on century-old homes. To the left is an old well, the bricks starting to give way to flowers.

The street transforms into a flower garden, where even Monet could have found inspiration for his paintings: it seems like part of another place, another time. In the summer it is inebriating. There's green everywhere, in window boxes, in large pots in front of the doors, and even on the ground, those tufts of grass rebelling against the stones. Among the fragrant blossoms, your nose finds itself in heaven and your mind lingers on the thought that pilgrims passed through this part of the "original" Via Francigena; I can't even imagine how different life on this street must have been amongst the precious metal stands and the gold merchants that populated this district and that of **Via dell'Oro.**

Another chill runs down my spine as I reach the end of the alleyway and come face to face with a beautiful tower house, catching a glimpse of its elegant terracotta water pipe on the left side, one of the last remaining examples of its times, as if I've just transported back into Etruscan times. A closed alley that opens your heart.

I love this part of the city, where you can go into alleys that, for no apparent reason, lead to nowhere. Like **Samoreci**, closed off on the right by the church of San Maurizio (distorted into Santo Moregi, which explains this strange name), or **Via di Finimondo** (World's end), which you can find by walking under the arch of San Maurizio (also known as the Romana bridge).

The poetry of Finimondo (World's end) is all a play on words. This street, right next to the church of Santo Spirito, runs right into the facade of a house. If you look closer, it seems that the only way out is through a ceramic tile depicting the Virgin Mary. She is the protagonist of this dead-end street, "adopted" by the Pispini district and transformed into the tabernacle for the *Nicchio Contrada*, decorated for the Feast Day celebrating the birth of the Virgin Mary on September 8. It seems that historically this street led to a small farm outside of the walls called "Finimondo." That's what I've been told, but let's keep the secret and the magic alive.

Wanting to hear nothing but the sound of my shoes, I search out **Vicolo di Pulcetino**, where I like to walk in silence and maybe stumble on the uneven bricks, the last remaining from the original pavement. This is yet another street that leads nowhere: but that's the beauty of it, letting yourself go, giving yourself a strange sense of freedom, that of who has no obligations to go anywhere. I envision the old farrier's shop (only the oldest residents of the neighborhood remember him), who assisted anyone wanting to shoe their horse before taking a walk into the countryside. If the "fleas" of the past don't make you wish for a cleaner place (filth reigned in this neighborhood), today you breathe in pleasant, natural scents and you may even forget we are in the center of the city.

I wander onto Via San Girolamo, in front of a historical bakery, the **Panificio di San Girolamo**. I look up at the first row of windows of the building in front of me and I notice another quirk: a *trompe-l'œil* of a window framing another window, in this case the real one. Gazing further up, in **Via delle Cantine** number 3, so many other windows create a false three-dimensional effect. A play on wedged glass and shudders inside painted frames: a sight that makes your head spin!

I know a lot of people that walk around without ever looking up, often so concentrated on the where they need to be that they never notice what they're missing. I prefer to observe, consider those details that elude most, those that make my imagination run. Otherwise, what kind of dreamer would I be?

You can see it in the weakness I have for windows: I try to pick up any details that let me imagine people's lives unfolding behind that glass. And here in town, there's so much to fantasize about! A young Sienese tried to court me in front of the **smallest window in the world**, at least that's how he put it. I have to confess that this discovery left me speechless: it wasn't its small size that shocked me, but rather the perfection of its shudders that rendered it a unique and rare beauty. I have to find it again, and I bet that the sight of it, even after so much time, has the same effect, even though this time I don't have that young man along with me.

Tracking it down won't be easy, but I'll remember the way. You begin in **Piazza Postierla** (or the *Quattro Cantoni*, four corners, as they call it here): a square constructed around the intersection of four streets, one of which is **Vicolo del Verchione** (an old Italian term meaning deadbolt, as this street was once closed off at night by a bolted door). Vicolo del Verchione is recognizable by its "rampant" arches, that connect one house to another. This is where the antique "*posterula*" would have been, later called "*postierla*", or "*piccola porta,*" small gate of the city walls. In fact, right next to it I find my small window, sitting up there on the left end of the first floor of the noble **Palazzo Chigi Piccolomini** (now local Arts, Cultural Heritage and Tourism offices). What a view they can enjoy, just by opening that miniature shudder! What sort of a "room with a view" is inside?

Now that I've had fun playing with windows that take my gaze elsewhere, I'm ready to continue daydreaming: do you remember the old artisan's shops, where our grandparents took us as kids? I go crazy for them. I have admired so many all over the streets in Siena. Here are some that have stayed with me:

ONCE UPON A TIME
Shops that Take you Back

Antica Drogheria Manganelli, Via di Città 71-73 (www.drogheria-manganelli.it, +39 0577 280002). A historic drug store first opened 140 years ago, where you can still smell the locally grown tarragon, and the aroma of homemade sweets, mostly *panforte*, a typical Sienese spice cake. Covering the store walls are original 19th century wooden shelving, a modern wonder, lined with jars full of herbs and drawers containing the best selection of Italian candies, inviting you to dive your hands in.

Pizzicheria De Miccoli in Via di Città 95 (+39 0577 289164): Local fresh deli. Everyone knows the owner Antonio for his famous mustache, and for that glasses-wearing boar's head hanging above the entrance welcoming you. You are now in the land of local cold cuts and cheese, served with a glass of wine posed on a couple of upside-down barrels used as tables, next to the characteristic Vicolo di Tone. This delicatessen, open since 1889, has seen more than its share of cured meats and cheeses hanging from the ceiling. You might accidentally hit your head on them, they hang right at eye level. If you've never tasted it, try the local *finocchiona* (typical Tuscan salami made with fennel seeds).

Ceramiche Santa Caterina in Via di Città 74 (+39 0577 283098): a historic artisanal ceramic shop, opened in the Fontebranda district in 1949. Now the shop is run by the Neri family, who houses their production in Via Mattioli, and the store in the center of the city, where you can find the most appealing original, hand painted creations, such as beautiful, Sienese style majolica (ceramic) inspired by themes and techniques used in the Duomo and the *contrade*.

Il Telaio in Chiasso del Bargello 2 (+39 0577 47065): The loom. In this artisanal laboratory, you can find handmade clothing and accessories made of high-quality fabrics like cashmere, cotton and silk. Every article is unique and weaved from the large loom welcoming visitors at the entrance.

Beads for beading in Via Monna Agnese, 12-14-16 (+39 335 6395758): in the historic heart of the city, behind the Duomo, you can still find traces of fossil remains found in Siena. A colorful studio of jewelry, gift ideas, lamps and furniture accessories made from Murano glass and local crystal, all created or chosen by the owner Silvia Tanganelli.

Panificio Il Magnifico in Via dei Pellegrini 27 (www.ilmagnifico.siena. it, +39 0577 281106): historic bakery at the foot of the palazzo Magnifico (Magnificent palace), from which it takes its name (home of the "Magnificent" Pandolfo Petrucci, governor of the Republic of Siena from 1472-1512). The family-run bakery opened in 1952 and safeguards the recipe for the best *pan co' santi* in the city (Sienese version of a sweet bread made with dried fruit and raisins, typical during the All-Saints holiday on November 1st). Don't try to get the owner Lorenzo Rossi to spill the beans, the perfect mix is up to him.

Erboristeria Amaranthus in Via di Diacceto 9 +39 0577 271180): Herbal medicine shop. The elegant sign "Erboristeria officinale" presents a true "healing oasis" where one can find many organic products for mind and body. A refined shop that has a second location in Via dei Pellegrini 4, the Profumeria Artistica e Naturale Amaranthus, that offers essential oils and elegant perfumes, among which *Terrae di Siena* (burnt Siena), as well as aromatherapy treatments.

Il Gomitolo in Via delle Terme 59 (www.ilgomitolonline.com; +39 0577 289306): a historic yarn and wool store just a few steps from Piazza del Campo. At the entrance an old scale and a 1920's mirror testify the original era of this shop: opened in 1924 as "Laneria Santi Guazzi" (or the "Casa della Lana", house of wool), in 2016 it changed both management and name, while keeping its passion intact and continuing to be a reference for anyone who loves knitting or crocheting.

Brocchi 1815 in Via del Porrione 41-43 (+39 347 4346393): Artisanal blacksmithing. In the bottom of the church of San Martino, a 19th century laboratory that keeps the "calderai" (local term for blacksmithing) tradition alive. Working among the bellows and coal forge are Laura Brocchi and her brother Alessandro (specialized in *repoussé* and wrought iron, respectively), the latest heirs of their family's Sienese tradition. The shop is full of historical pieces: armor and arms as well as objects for the Palio that are still used in the historic parade. A multitude of splendid creations are for sale, ranging from contemporary design to *Art Nouveau.*

Biciclette Bianchi in Via Camollia 206 (📞 +39 0577 48306): the last bicycle repair shop in Siena, where the heirs of the Rossi family, historic "bicycle mechanics" since 1953, continue to sell helmets, apparel and anything that cycling lovers will need. On special request by enthusiasts, they will open their small museum in Via Roma 1, where they keep old tools, such as hand drills, liberty style plates, legendary team jerseys (Legnano, Torpado, Arbos). Black and white photographs on the walls, one in particular depicting the unforgettable starts of the *Giro d'Italia* in 1952 with Bartali and Coppi.

Casa delle pelle in Via Camollia 153 (🔗 www.sienahandmadeleatherbags.com, 📞 +39 0577 287475): workshop and store opened in 1985 by Paolo Infunti creates handmade leather goods like wallets, belts and purses in every shape, size and color. Displayed along with his leather creations are costumes and medieval arms. Be careful when you move around inside the shop, you wouldn't want to make a lance or suit of armor fall!

Il ciabattino in Via Mattioli 1: Shoe repair shop. Once you enter into Roberto's minuscule shop with no sign, rare tools such as cobbler's punches, knives and wooden forms surround you. It will make you remember the "good old times" when prices were written by hand on pieces of paper, measurements taken on cardboard boxes and artisans that knew how to repair shoes weren't such a rarity.

The fact that some old signs are still hanging and some artists resist modernity is additional proof of Siena's ancient soul. For this reason, I allow myself to explore some more "gems" with just enough time to find that romantic gift for myself.

La **Fabbrica delle Candele** (Via dei Pellegrini 11, 🔗 www.lafabbricadellecandele.com, 📞 +39 0577 289179) is an artisanal candle-making workshop. Right in the shop Anna and the other artists shape wonderful wax flowers and candles, as well as hand painted items depicting Tuscan landscapes with cypress trees or sunflowers, so you can leave with a "piece" of Sienese countryside. They can also personalize gifts with a name or dedication.

Not far from there is the **Manufactus** (Via di Città 37, 📞 0577 284241), that makes you want to put pen to this exquisite paper, dirtying your hands with ink just to have had the pleasure of writing a letter and breathing in that special smell. Here you can also take a marbling class, and learn how to decorate paper through patterns of color resembling marble. For those, like me, who love this medium, find it exhilarating leaving traces of your own thoughts on such a special paper, and inspiring to see what poetry they become!

If you're still feeling creative, let's walk a little bit more, to Via di Beccheria, the **Alvalenti Humor Gallery** (🔊 www.alvalenti.com) is waiting for us. Inside you can find drawings and prints both small and large, all following the unique vision of Alessandro Valenti. A Valenti drawing is perfect for dreamers of all ages that want to transform their walls and dive into a fantastic and colorful illustration of the city.

Another art studio worth slipping into is the **Galleria Novecento**, in Via di Pantaneto 63 (📞 +39 333 8231512): prints, signs, posters of Italian and international masterpieces from the last century, antique objects that evoke memories, images and sensations of the past.

Yet another stop to make is at **La Mobille** (🔊 www.lamobille.it, 📞 +39 0577 052083) in Via Camollia 126, a workshop that revives antique furniture for sustainable reuse: chests, hat boxes, lamps and other objects found become original creations in Camilla's hands, as she transforms them into one of a kind pieces to experience first-hand.

How could we do Charles Dickens wrong? If Venice is the ideal city for losing oneself, Siena isn't far behind. Not among the canals, rather among the countless shops and medieval streets, sometimes hidden from sight, ready to surprise us.

At this exact moment, the rest of the day is a poetic anticipation of the night: the moon begins to show in the horizon. I start envisioning a party in the **Loggia della Mercanzia**, called the *Casin de' Nobili* that is home to the *Circolo degli Uniti*, considered the oldest gentleman's club in Europe, founded in 1657. I don't have time to go

THE MARKET IN PIAZZA DEL CAMPO

One winter day I happened to run into an extraordinary sight. Was I dreaming or was it real? The shell of Piazza del Campo filled with lights, Christmas decorations, wooden stands, flavors, colors and aromas. I find myself walking among homegrown vegetables, handmade objects, local herbs and spices: it's the magic of the **Market in Piazza del Campo** held the first weekend of December, transforming the **piazza** into one of the most fascinating markets in Italy.

Five hundred stands, local handmade fabrics, products and food; specialties from around Italy. For a sentimental person like me it's the perfect moment to dive into the history of the **Campo**. I envision farmers and craftsmen coming in from the countryside after a long and trying trip to display their goods on the great stage that is this **piazza**. Times have certainly changed, but it's satisfying to relive these poetic moments, where the living room of Siena becomes a "garden" of seasonal harvest and a "community" for welcoming pilgrims from all over.

Lovers of handmade goods will feel back on their honeymoon: hand-blown glass, handmade wool and paper objects, wrought iron accessories, jewelry, hand-painted ceramics. So many flavors from the **Bel Paese**, this beautiful country: fresh pasta, cheese, cured meats, olive oil, not to mention delicacies such as saffron, honey, herbs like calamint (a Mediterranean herb of the mint family that can be used for flavoring meat, fish and vegetables, often artichokes). There's usually an area reserved for children's games and a few "corners" under the Torre del Mangia dedicated to two passions: wine and reading.

in, this isn't the 15th century and I don't have the right dress on. More importantly, I wouldn't want to miss the sweetest moment of the day, sunset. I go back towards the **Basilica dei Servi**, already pink from the lights of the *Valdimontone Contrada*. It's hard to find words to describe it: just go up the stairs that lead to the entrance landing then turn around. The look of magic in your eyes will say enough: they are drowning in a sea of green hills on the horizon, the shadow of the Duomo's tower, the merlons of the Palazzo Pubblico in contrast, set in an orange frame.

This is the most romantic view of the city, lined with cypress trees, in which the *Torre* touches the sky, yet at the same time seems so close I reach my hand out as if to touch it. I breathe in this crisp air, in this eternal moment, waiting as the light continues to fade.

Now that's it's evening, it's a good idea to let the lights of one of the *contrade* guide you. I recommend you follow the **braccialetti**, *contrada* bracelets. What were you thinking? You won't find them on *contrada* member's wrists but hanging high on doors and windows. They are a type of streetlight made of carved wood, and decorated with the colors and emblems of the *contrada*, used for lighting the streets of the district during its *Festa Titolare*, a yearly celebration of its Patron Saint, from May to September, or during the four days of the Palio. I adore them. The streets become so romantic. This is how the *contrade* decorate for their festivities, putting on their "Sunday best" made of flags blowing in the wind, warm lights and ardent choruses: a perfect symphony of passion, art and beauty. How can one not fall in love here!

At the end of this long walk through my memories, I would like to show you one last place you have to "taste;" as they say in Latin *Dulcis in fondo*, leaving the sweetest part for last. What better way than to end the day on a sweet note, in Via Porta Giustizia 11, at the Tea Room.

THE TEA ROOM
indulge in Ilario's desserts

In a corner of **Piazza del Mercato**, with a view of the Porta Giustizia valley, a long stairwell hides this place of the past from indiscreet eyes. Let's go down the stairs of the **Tea Room** by leaving our modern-day worries behind us. Right outside the door we are thrown into another time and space by an antique telescope.

As we cross the threshold, we look around curiously: books on old shelves, a heart-warming fireplace in front of a welcoming sofa. Dim lights, wooden jewels, cabinets hanging onto the rock wall, precious lace, welcoming niches, a few musical instruments, pictures and paintings everywhere.

The piano dominates the small, raised space similar to a stage; a desirable object to the eyes of enthusiasts, and work desk for the notes of many professional musicians that delight the place with their performances in jazz or other themed evenings. This place is full of surprises: one night I even ran into the director Giovanni Veronesi, improvising music and verses from a famous Francesco Nuti song at the piano until dawn.

Evenings at the Tea Room pass slowly, with good music, book presentations and blues sessions. The common thread is the sweet noise of spoons turning in tea pots, the soul of this place. The teacups, all different, are personally chosen according to the personality of the guest: who's more classic, who likes to experiment. Ilario Bondani, the historical and enthusiastic owner, will try to interpret the nature and humor of his clients, mixing it all with his innate know-how and his famous question: "Would you like to hear about this evening's desserts?"

Choose between a homemade cake and a relaxing herbal tea, a chocolate cake and a "dreaming of love" infusion. There's something for everyone here: we can look for love, forge unexpected friendships, or, who knows, discover a new travel companion. The Tea Room never disappoints; home to Erasmus students, tourists, loafers, and many Sienese looking to be pampered.Inaugurated more than 30 years ago, in 1985, the Tea Room never goes out of style, thanks to its winning recipe: time seems to stop and hours to fly by without notice. I look at the clock and it's already two o'clock in the morning, almost closing time, but it's my last night here in this splendid city and I decide, for once, to abandon the daily rush and fully enjoy my Sienese "Night in Tibet," my favorite herbal tea. How I wish it would never end…

I fall into a deep sleep. When I wake up in my comfortable bed I am still reminiscing about that little corner where I lost myself in another era, forgetting, if only for a few hours, the frenzy of our times. As soon as I can, I promise myself to go back there. With that telescope waiting for us on the landing it's never too early, or too late, to go out and "see – once more - the stars[1]".

P.S. Unfortunately you can't seek out the Tea Room in the summer months, as it closes for the whole season. During the other months, I recommend making a reservation (☎ +39 0577 222753)!

---

1   Dante Alighieri, *The Divine Comedy, Inferno*, XXXIV, 139, translated from the original *"a riveder le stelle"* (https://digitaldante.columbia.edu/dante/divine-comedy/inferno/inferno-34/)

Walking through Time

For the scholar stopping in Siena

Derived from the Greek *xénia* (small gifts given to house guests), from the Etruscan *sana* (health) or the religious term *sinua* (curve, taken at an intersection): I scan the pages of historical manuals and I can't find a definitive answer. The etymology of the name Siena remains obscure.

Legend has it that Siena is the daughter of Rome. Founded by Senius, son of Remus, forced to escape with his brother Aschius from the rage of his Uncle Romulus, who had killed their father. The first twin founded Siena, settling in *Castel Senio* (an area now called Castelvecchio, old castle) bringing with himself the statue of the She-wolf, the latter establishing the city of Asciano.

Let's get things clear: a studious girl like me doesn't believe in myths like this. I only trust historical sources! And so, digging further in some books, the most trustworthy explanation seems to involve an aristocratic Etruscan family, the *Sainas or Seinas*, probably related to the Saenia family, Roman senators. The Romans were also responsible for the founding of the city; after an Etruscan settlement (VI century B.C.), followed by Gaulish control (the Senones, IV century B.C.), they built a military colony called *Senia Julia* (1st century B.C.).

Up to this point in history we have to trust the authoritative stories of Pliny the Elder (*Naturalis Historia*) and Tacitus (*Historiae*), but also the late Roman Empire's Road atlas (*Tabula Peutigeriana*).

Confirming this theory is the findings of ceramics, amphoras and urns still visible today in the **National Archaeological Museum** inside the Santa Maria della Scala.

Now that we finally have some history under our belt, we can start our viaticus, a tour rediscovering the past. Let's start, then, from the roots of the *Castel Senio*, where everything began: **Via di Castelvecchio** is the street we see rise up from Via San Pietro, and that small and challenging slope upwards prepares us for an unexpected vision.

Veering to the right, a series of steps leads us to a timeless courtyard: four sides of homes set together, similar to a protected castle, the first traces of the transformation of Siena from village to *oppidum*, a fortified area set on the highest part of the city, dominating the surrounding countryside.

The lattice of adjacent streets draws out a sort of oval that hypothetically retraces the first walls of the military settlement: walking along it searching out **Vicolo di Castelvecchio** on our left at the fork of Via di Castelvecchio we end up in **Via Tommaso Pendola**, formerly called Via della Murella, small wall street: the spot where the old walls reached, a path from Via San Pietro to the Quattro Cantoni that went left from Via Stalloreggi to Pian dei Mantellini, and ended in Via di San Quirico.

It's easy to imagine a fortified castle within this circle, especially if you observe the marks on the walls. Let's challenge ourselves to find the hidden corner of **Via del Contino**, a small dead end street right after **Piazza del Conte**: we end up right in front of a large, pointy and asymmetric stone wall, remains of the old **muraglia di Castelvecchio**, the walls surrounding Castelvecchio (where now you can see the tabernacle of the *Pantera Contrada*, by painter Enzo Pollai). If that's not enough, another irrefutable remnant is the **Torre di Voltaia**, Voltaia family tower, that you can see by looking up to the right: today it seems cut off (maybe because of the 1798 earthquake) and right below this street once met up with Via di Castelvecchio.

Throughout my studies I remember well that this was supposed to be the first district of the city, seat of the magistrates of the Roman colony. Then, as occurred in all Western countries, centuries of the

Dark Ages followed until the Barbaric invasions and the Gothic War. During Lombard occupation in the 6th century, it was a residence for local administrative and judicial officials, or gastalds. Towards the end of the 8th century it was a residence for counts and viscounts of the Frank domination of Charlemagne's Holy Roman Empire. The first document confirming the existence of the castle is from the year 1010: a lease to the Count Siena Bernard, stipulated in the Viscount Guido's home *"ad locus ad castello vetero,"* the location of the old castle.

The idea of *castrum vetus*, old castle, is legitimate proof of the new city that was emerging. Right in front of me, at the end of Via San Pietro, I catch sight of **Porta all'Arco**, that marked the new borders of the city walls during the 11th and 12th centuries. From there the walls extended to the right passing through **Via delle Cerchia** and connected the **Arco di Santa Lucia** (**Santa Lucia Arch**) with the **two gates, Due Porte**. On the other side, the walls continued along **Via Sant'Agata** until reaching the **Porta di San Salvatore**, that still today elegantly "frames" the steep **Via Duprè**: a necessary widening of the wall circumference due to population growth and urban drift from the countryside.

This rapid digression mustn't leave out the spread of Christianity around Siena, most likely around 4th century C.E. We know that Siena became an official diocese halfway through the fifth century and Castelvecchio surely was the bishops' residence, maybe even location of the cathedral. Among the many possibilities, the most valid seems to locate the first Duomo in the area of the current **Santa Margherita church and convent** (incorporated in the rooms of the ex-Tommaso Pendola Institute for the Deaf).

Getting back to the facts: until the 9th century temporal power (counts appointed by the Empire) and spiritual power (bishops nominated by the Pope) coexisted in an unstable balance. From the 11th century the Santa Maria hill became the fulcrum of the city: today's Duomo was constructed there, and right in front of the Duomo the monumental **Santa Maria della Scala** hospital (today a museum) was established as a place of solace for the bodies and minds of traveling pilgrims.

Who were these traveling pilgrims? In one of my manuals I read that the historian Ernesto Sestan defines Siena as a "daughter of the street." Urban development and the city's fortune are closely tied to the **Via Francigena** that passed through its center: given this name because it came directly from France, following a path connecting the most crucial and sacred Christian sights. To the north Canterbury, Besançon, Reims e Calais; to the west Santiago de Compostela; Rome to the south and, by sea from the ports of Puglia: Jerusalem and Palestine.

An itinerary for pilgrims that cut Siena in two and allowed for the gradual incorporation of the citizens of the hills that until that moment were left on the margins of the city: we can find traces of this at the beginning of **Via dei Termini**, looking up at the travertine crests hanging on the facades of three buildings, that indicate respectively the three territories, or *Terzi* (thirds), into which the city was divided, and their further subdivision in *contrade* (attested by documents from the end of the 12th century nominating *the contrada de termine*, official *contrada* borders). On the pavement, gleaming plates reveal that that is the where the *Terzi* meet (*Città, Camollia* and *San Martino*).

The **Terzo di Città** is the original nucleus of Castelvecchio, extended to the Santa Maria hill and reaching Via di Città: the art historian Cesare Brandi defined it as the Sienese "Acropolis"; beating heart where you can still find the most ancient buildings.

I want to tread on the Via Francigena, to retrace a part of its path. At the northern end of the city, the **Terzo di Camollia** welcomes us. Along Via Camollia, Via dei Montanini and Banchi di Sopra we stroll past the residences of the two most powerful families: **Rocca Salimbeni** (actual headquarters of the Monte dei Paschi di Siena bank) and **Palazzo Tolomei** (13th century). At the end of Banchi di Sopra, home of bankers and rich merchants, with banchi referring to the business of exchanging money), we find ourselves at a fork that tests our sense of direction.

The name says it all, we are at the **Croce del Travaglio** (named after a certain Scarsello del Travaglio, attested in a document from

1150). At the time it mustn't have been so difficult to choose the right direction, as it seems there was an old cross with three cardinal directions on it, orienting pilgrims to the left on **Banchi di Sotto**. This is how Banchi di Sotto became part of the **Terzo di San Martino**, where from the 8th century the church of the same name, protector of travelers and pilgrims, was erected. The street continues straight down skimming the noteworthy **Castellare deli Ugurgieri** on the left (another important Sienese noble family), and Piazza del Campo on the right.

Passing the University of Siena's main building, on the other side of the street two elegant Renaissance buildings show off: **Palazzo Piccolomini**, named after the Sienese family, and the **Logge del Papa (Loggia of the Pope)**, with the dedication in Latin on the architrave of Pope Pius II, at the time still Enea Silvio Piccolomini: "*gentilibus suis picolomineis,*" family of Piccolomini.

After Via Pantaneto is Via Roma: passing under our feet is the way to the "Eternal City," under the San Maurizio arch (known by Sienese as the **Ponte di Romana**, or Romana bridge, once the gate of San Maurizio al Ponte, complete with a lifting gate) and continuing out the **Porta Romana**.

Moving past the *Terzi*, we can pick up our historical narration with the conflict between two absolute powers, even though we know how it ends: a 150 year-long battle between Guelphs (Pope supporters) and Ghibellines (those loyal to the Emperor), and the exhaustive battle for territory between Siena and her archenemy Florence. Things aren't always as they seem, however, in many periods the Sienese sided (for convenience) with one or the other faction. It was interesting for me to read that mid-12th century Siena supported the Emperor Frederick I of Sweden (Redbeard) and not their "own" pope, Sienese Alexander III; but as they say, all is fair in love and war...

In the meanwhile, the city had transformed into "Comune" (attested in a legal dispute in 1125 between the Diocese of Siena and Arezzo), held by the collective magistrate of the *consoli* (consuls, a group of magistrates belonging to the oldest families in the city), to which was given the deciding power for war, peace and justice. Collaborating with them were the bishops on all patrimonial, juridical and notary deeds.

Right away the City created administrative bodies that acted for centuries, such as the "Campana," meaning bell, a general counsel called to order by the sound of the San Cristoforo church bell, and the office of the *Biccherna*, financial magistrate. For a period of time the consul began to alternate with a new figurehead called the *podestà*, or mayor, supported by the *Capitano del Popolo*, Captain of the People, whose founding in 1235 represented a true political transformation. The *Capitaneus Populi senensis*, Captain of the Sienese people, recognizable by a white, crowned lion on a red crest, represented the new political group "of the people," an extended bourgeoisie, that elected half of the representatives of the new *Governo dei Ventiquattro*, Government of Twenty-four (a counsel of 24 elected officials) founded in 1240.

The birth of the **Università degli Studi di Siena**, one of the oldest universities in Europe, occurred at the same time. The mayor of the city in 1240, Cacciaconti, issued a decree revealing the direct involvement of the City in the organization of the study courses: a city tax funded the instructors of the *Studium Universitatis Senarum* (*latin*: University of Siena), that originally was composed of schools of law, grammar and medicine. This institution was also named the University of the Holy Roman Empire during the reign of Charles IV; and in 1416 summoned scholars from all over Italy to its new *Casa della Sapienza*, House of Wisdom, in the rooms of a previous charitable institution, *Domus Misericordiae* in Via della Sapienza, the Street of Wisdom.

We've drawn close to an important historical date for Siena: September 4, 1260, the **Battle of Montaperti**. For many Sienese this is the moment in which Siena's history truly begins; here emerges the independent spirit that defines what it means to "be Sienese." It is a pride that you can perceive on the streets, that boldly echoes the expression "Republic of Siena," referring to that long period (over 400 years) in which the city was an independent state, from Gualfredo's deposing in 1125 as the last reigning bishop, until 1555, the fall of the city to the Duchy of Florence.

Those epic verses that immortalized this battle come to mind: "The carnage, the great bloodshed /That stained the waters of the Arbia red."[1] The Arbia is a river that flows through Montaperti, just a few kilometers from Siena, stage of a clash that left hundreds of victims and that saw the glorious victory by the Sienese deployed by King Manfred of Sicily, Frederick II of Sweden's son, against the Florentine Guelphs. Victory was attained thanks to the Virgin Mary's divine intervention, which is why Siena from that moment on would be called *Sena Vetus Civitas Virginis* (Siena, City of the Virgin).

Making the news for his honorable valor in this battle was **Provenzano Salvani,** to whom Dante dedicated several verses, memorialized in two plaques in the city. "'Provenzan Salvani,'/ he answered, 'here because – presumptuously-'/ he thought his grip could master all Siena.[2]" We find this introduction to Salvani in Via del Moro, where his residences once were. He was a member of the Government of Twenty-four who ends up in Purgatory's terrace of pride by accruing too much power and thus nominating himself "Lord of Siena."

In Piazza del Campo, at the **bocca del Casato (Mouth of the Casato**), where the Casato di Sotto street pours into the *piazza*, recalls another episode: "Then of his own free will he set/aside all shame and took his place upon/the *Campo* of Siena."[3] Dante recalls how Provenzano demonstrated generosity towards a friend taken prisoner by Charles of Anjou in the Battle of Tagliacozzo. With bail set at 10,000 Florins, Salvani shamelessly begged the city for the

---

1   Dante Alighieri, *The Divine Comedy, Inferno*, X, 85-86, translated from the original "*Lo strazio e 'l grande scempio che fece l'Arbia colorata in rosso*" (https://digitaldante.columbia.edu/dante/divine-comedy/inferno/inferno-10/)

2   Dante Alighieri, *The Divine Comedy, Purgatory* XI, 121-123, translated from the original "*Quelli è, rispuose, Provenzan Salvani; ed è qui perché fu presuntuoso a recar Siena tutta a le sue mani*" (https://digitaldante.columbia.edu/dante/divine-comedy/purgatorio/purgatorio-11/)

3   Dante Alighieri, *The Divine Comedy, Purgatory* XI, 134-135, translated from the original "*Liberamente nel Campo di Siena, ogni vergogna deposta, s'affisse*" (https://digitaldante.columbia.edu/dante/divine-comedy/purgatorio/purgatorio-11/)

money by laying down his cloak in the *piazza*. Although he behaved nobly this time, he still ended up amongst the proud.

As we know, Dante didn't look kindly on the Sienese, as proven when he asks Virgilio, his guide throughout his voyage in the underworld, the most classic rhetorical questions: "Was there ever/So vain a people as the Sienese?"[4] It's fun to follow the path laid out by the eight plaques dedicated to Dante's verses scattered throughout the historical center (posted in 1921), through which his characters come alive.

We've already found two of them, but in order to continue our treasure hunt and find the others we'll need some clues. The verses dedicated to two Sienese women are near Piazza Tolomei: **Pia de' Tolomei** is the protagonist of **Vicolo della Torre**, placed among the negligent souls in Purgatory who repented only at the time of their sudden, violent deaths; while **Sapìa Salvani**, Provenzano's aunt, is remembered in both **Via Vallerozzi** and **Vicolo Pier Pettinaio** (name of the beatified, celebrated comb seller who, praying for Sapìa's soul, that saved her from Inferno but didn't excuse her from the Envious circle of Purgatory). For the other plaques, look in **Vicolo del Tiratoio**, where it's easy to run into romantic souls; or go on a "hunt" for Garibaldi (**Via Garibaldi**); you could also take a walk, just like our eternal child, in **Via della Diana**, for an event shrouded in mystery.

Let's go back to the series of events following the Battle of Montaperti: the Sienese army was defeated in the battles of Benevento (1266), Tagliacozzo (1268) and Colle Val d'Elsa (1269 - where our war hero Provenzano Salvani died), marking the end of the Ghibelline government, and making way for the **Guelph Government of the Nine** in 1287. Elected by the bankers and city merchants (also known as magnates) the Nine alternated power every two months, upheld by a principle of rotation that should have guaranteed balance, equality and the search for the Good of All.

This was the beginning of a golden age for Siena, considered its

---

4 Dante Alighieri, *The Divine Comedy*, *Interno* XXIX, 121-122, translated from the original "*Or fu già mai gente sì vana come la sanese?*" (https://digitaldante.columbia.edu/dante/divine-comedy/inferno/inferno-29/)

years of maximum splendor until 1355. Piazza del Campo already existed, as the City had bought the grounds in 1169 for 20 lire, but with the Nine it completely changed aesthetic: today we can still admire the **nine slices** that divide the internal shell, each one dedicated to one of the governors of the city.

Later on came the **Fonte Gaia** and the construction of the **Palazzo Pubblico** (still housing Siena's city hall). One of its most notable rooms, the one dedicated to the Nine, is home to the *Allegory of Good and Bad Government* by Ambrogio Lorenzetti: a frescoed masterpiece that represents, through art, the good works of the new government.

Then there is the **Torre del Mangia**, built between 1338-1349 as a political attempt to match the height of the cathedral's bell tower, all the while starting from a geographically lower point. On the Tower and the Palazzo Pubblico you can notice square Guelph merlons; by order of the Nine, all the Ghibelline merlons (swallow-tailed) were to disappear from the buildings of the city.

If we are looking for more intriguing evidence of the past, from Via di Città take a look into the **Vicolo di Tone** by crossing a suggestive passageway that leads to **Via dei Percennesi**. Turning to the right, we find ourselves under two elegant symmetrical arches, it's the perfect moment to turn around. Gazing upwards we notice a series of swallow-tailed merlons that top the historic Palazzo Marescotti, famous Ghibelline family residence.

Take a moment to consider that we are on the backside of the actual **Palazzo Chigi Saracini**, whose facade is framed by **horizontal Guelph merlons**, sign of the new political direction: in just a few seconds, moving a few meters from the back to the front of a building, we have traveled across an entire century of history.

Had those Ghibelline merlons, almost hidden from sight, been forgotten by the Nine? Not at all. They appear in their original form thanks to a restoration effort in the 20th century that removed the newer Guelph construction.

THE STATE ARCHIVES

Looking for living proof of the past, I allow myself a stop at the **State Archives**, inside Palazzo Piccolomini in Banchi di Sotto. There I can touch first-hand priceless works of art and historical documents.

The **Museo delle Biccherne (Biccherne Museum)**, *in primis*: a collection of 105 *biccherne*, or wooden covers of the City of Siena's financial magistrate's oldest financial records, dating from 1258 through mid-18th century. Masterpieces by the likes of Ambrogio Lorenzetti, Vecchietta, and Rustichino, that illustrate five centuries of history, and follow three principal iconographic themes: writing, religion and politics. The rest of the museum is dedicated to an enormous collection **of historical documents**: decorated manuscripts, parchments, Papal stamps, and imperial diplomas that span from the year 735 A.D. to the Unification of Italy in 1861.

Here is a list of some of the most important and/or intriguing:

- the first **Constitution** of the Republic of Siena, early 14th century, written in "vulgar" (spoken Italian of the time, as opposed to Latin) and adopted by the Government of the Nine;

- the **bookkeeping of the Santa Maria della Scala hospital**, in antique volumes and consultable;

- **fine given to the poet Cecco Angiolieri** (July 13, 1282): 20 coins for being caught wandering the streets at night after the third bell (approximately 10:00p.m.);

- writings on the most important Sienese saints, such as the **code of San Bernardino** (1442) and the Official Stamp of Pope Pius II (1461) in which he proclaims the **canonization of St. Catherine of Siena**;

- a **Dantean collection**, with documents on characters of the Divine Comedy or people who are in someway tied to the Supreme Poet, such as the **will of Giovanni Boccaccio** (1374);

- **"the list of useless mouths,"** people forced out of the city under Spanish siege in 1554 because they were old, sick, or orphaned, and sentenced to certain death (one of the most difficult moments of the Republic of Siena).

During the Government of the Nine's rule, the construction of the last perimeter wall began and is still standing (the last gate, Porta Tufi, was inaugurated in 1425); the construction site of the colossal project of the new Duomo also began. In **Piazza Jacopo della Quercia** we can still find hard to ignore traces of the incomplete original structure, seeming to be the facade of a church. In fact, that's what it was supposed to be, as documented in 1339 after a deliberation and approval for expansion of the Duomo by the "Campana" Consul.

What's left of that "big" dream today are the columns of what would have been the three naves, a door on the left side (that leads to the Baptistery) and the facade, known as the **Facciatone**, or large facade. The project was never successfully carried out due to structural issues and the arrival of the **Black Plague**, a disease that decimated the population.

It was the year 1348 and in just a few months about half of the population died (at that time the population of Siena was around 50,000, the same size of Paris!), a true breaking point in the history of the city. Siena was halved in strength, and, even more debilitated after the second wave of the epidemic in 1374, was forced to drastically limit its aspirations of glory.

Then, in March of 1355, the most important ruling figures of the Republic (Mayor, Captain of the People and Captain of War) were chased out of the city by the arrival of the Roman Emperor Charles IV's troops.

Moving forward in time, we come across an important document. It is now preserved in the **Rocca Salimbeni** and attests to the foundation of the oldest bank in the world: on February 27, 1472 the "Monte di Pietà" or "Monte Pio" (Mountain of Pity or Pious) was born. In 1624 the name was changed to **Monte dei Paschi**, its current name, as the earnings from the Maremma region's pastures were used as a guarantee.

This brings us quickly to the 16th century, when Siena decided to align with the Emperor, a period of time now remembered as the **Battle of Camollia** (1526), won against the much larger military sent from Pope Clement VII and the Florentines, who were pushed back all the way to Palazzo Diavoli, a building still standing outside of Porta Camollia. Under the rule of the Roman Emperor Charles V, Siena was consequently under Spanish dominion, occupied by Governor Don Diego Hurtado de Mendoza's troops for some time until a revolt momentarily expelled the foreign troops. This **popular uprising** in 1552 is monumentalized on an epigraph at Porta Tufi, celebrating the achievements of the expelled Sienese who guided the uprising.

This victory didn't last long, however, as the city was then seized by Imperial and Medicean troops. One of these epic moments occurred right in Via Biagio di Montluc, where a plaque commemorates the "heroic Sienese women" who defended the freedom of their homeland: the resistance ended in 1555, date marking the official surrender of the **Republic of Siena.**

The end of Sienese independence coincides with Medici family rule. Cosimo I, having to manage this new State (**Siena**), kept it separate from the old State (**Florence**). An institutional dualism that can be found in a beautiful *palazzo* in Piazza Duomo, to the right of the cathedral: the **Palazzo del Governatore (the Governor's Hall)**, seat of the new central ducal power, set to assist the Sienese magistrates left in charge in the Palazzo Pubblico. Cosimo I's reign also achieved regional unity and led to the birth of the Granduchy of Tuscany (1569).

After the Medicean dynasty, in 1765 power passed to the Habsburg Lorraine empire and to **Leopold II**, the enlightened prince, and then briefly to the French occupation of the city in 1796, as well as Napoleonic domination.

Let's take a quick step backwards, so we can hear about the origins of the Palio: August 15, 1581, seven knights representing respective *contrade*, take part in a race from the Church in Valli (outside of Porta Romana) to the cathedral, in celebration of the Assumption of the Virgin Mary. We are at the "roots" of an event, the Palio, that has been celebrated since then, changing its rules but not its spirit, personifying the essence of the city: tradition, festivities, devotion, culture, belonging. There's all this and more in the *contrade*, a territorial grouping of people that has been fixed since the famous **decree by Violante di Baviera.** On September 13, 1729 the Governess of Siena approved the division of the territory of Siena into 17 *contrade*, thus establishing the precise borders of the different districts and authorizing a ban on introducing new ones. A decree relevant even for us today, the cornerstone of the Palio and its centuries-long history.

Before we get to the 20th century, there is one last important marking on the walls of the city. *"O Roma viene all'Italia, o l'Italia va a Roma"* (Either Rome comes to Italy, or Italy goes to Rome) is the epigraph displayed on Banchi di Sopra, between numbers 27 and 29. These are the words of **Giuseppe Garibaldi**, pronounced on August 11, 1867 from what was once called the Aquila Nera Hotel. Down below, near Piazza Tolomei, an entire city applauding him. News writings recall his arrival by train, dressed in the Redshirts uniform, accompanied by 400 volunteers, immersed in a crowd of over 25,000: a historic moment immortalized in the city. Another lesser-known trace of the general is kept in the historical archives of the Monte dei Paschi Bank. A letter dated November 26, 1875, addressed to the tax collector in Rome and signed by his hand that states very frankly: *"Sig. Esattore, mi trovo nell'impossibilità di pagare imposte"* (Mr. Collector, I find it impossible for me to pay taxes).

We have now come upon the arrival of modernity and its encounter with rural tradition, as the Sienese writer **Federigo Tozzi** illustrates in his novels *Con gli occhi chiusi* (*With Closed Eyes*, 1919), *Tre croci* (*Three Crosses*, 1920) and Il podere (1921). Siena couldn't not be the protagonist of his pages, place of "clashes" between city and countryside, a deep look into the existential condition of its characters.

And just like that, our time jump into history has flown, and my mind with it. I'm looking for a way to get back to modern times and I run straight into the three historical Sienese *Accademie*, still today active cultural centers: the scientific academy, **I Fisiocritici;** literature academy, **Accademia degli Intronati;** and the **Accademia dei Rozzi**, known for its theater.

A COLLECTION OF MUSICAL NOTES

I turn back up Via di Città and I can't help but notice the suggestive profile of **Palazzo Chigi Saracini**. This time it's not the architecture that draws me closer, but the music that I hear coming from inside. I peek in and see a caffè in the courtyard. In front of a cup of tea, I reflect on the fact that much of the richness within these walls is both precious yet intangible. The Count Guido, worldly man and lover of beauty, had the intuition and generosity to gather together the best teachers and performers in the world, founding the **Accademia Chigiana di Siena**. Still to this day prestigious summer courses are held for a very selective group of young artists.

I realize that the concerts of Count Guido's students were truly *avant-garde*. It's not open to tours right now, but I remember being told that the *Accademia* possesses a collection of rare volumes of music, so the library may just be open. I take the stairs and ring the bell. The heavy door opens slowly and a nice man greets me. "Of course, the library is open, please come in." As I climb the stairs, I see several closed doors: who knows what treasures are hiding behind them and what the Count had intended them for. I will have to find out the guided tour schedule: there must be a collection of countless marvels in this building (www.chigiana.org). After the first ramp I peek into a door left ajar: it's the **Salone dei Concerti**, concert hall, a gem in rococo style with white stucco and golden friezes. I perceive the presence of an organ up high, nestled in a splendid choir that wraps the perimeter of the room. Due to its oval shape the acoustics here must be exceptional. I continue to climb and I reach a corridor where an enormous family tree of the Chigi Saracini family is hung; just a bit further down the hall is the door to the library.

There is a person at the table consulting a score: I sit nearby and he begins to talk to me. He tells me some anecdotes about the Count and how important he was, not only in the international music field, but also locally. He also proudly tells me that he himself is a member of the oldest choir in Siena, founded by Chigi himself in 1935, merging two already established choirs, called the **Unione Corale Senese**. The choir is still very active today. He invites me to visit them, which he assures me is worth it. I wouldn't miss an occasion like this, seeing as it's just a close walk away in Via Pendola 41.

Santa Margherita in the Calstelvecchio district is one of the few baroque churches in Siena, later incorporated into the Pendola building. To enter one must contact the Choir and make an appointment (www.unionecoralesenese.it). The *Madonna Nera*, the black Virgin on the left altar, is enthralling. My guide's face lights up as he explains to me that right in the rows of this choir the great **Ettore Bastianini**, world-famous baritone, was born. Sienese to the core, he was also captain of the *Pantera Contrada*.

The story of the life of Bastianini fascinates me to the point that I decide to pursue the traces of another artist who sold out box offices: Francesco Bernardi. Nicknamed **il Senesino** (little Sienese), Francesco was one of the most famous *castrato* singers of the mid-18th century, searched out even by Haendel. His original home has since been inherited by distant descendants and is one of the buildings with its entrance in **Via dei Montanini** that looks out over the Lizza gardens. I try to figure out which one it is: it can't be any other than the blue one on the corner of **Vicolo dello Sportello**.

I head to the nearby **Fortezza (fortress)**. The ex-military barracks is now occupied by two local music organizations: the Siena Jazz Foundation, a prestigious school with an international program of concerts and shows (www.sienajazz.it) and the **Banda Città del Palio**, the city's marching band, that accompanies the contrade throughout the city during their yearly celebrations playing Siena's anthem (www. bandacittadelpalio.it).

My ears perk up as I hear different notes intertwine, a mix of piano jazz and drum beats. Such a blend of melodies that seem to perfectly embody Siena.

I think back to that intriguing motto at Via di Città 36, the entrance to the **Accademia dei Rozzi**: *"chi qui soggiorna acquista quel che perde"* (He who stays here acquires that which he loses). What can be lost with culture? I should have thought of it earlier: ignorance! I wonder if this could be true for me: I also tried to lose ignorance in my visit to Siena, searching for the "scars" of an indelible past through walls, streets and buildings that brought me back to their origins.

Margaret Youcenar wrote in *Memoirs of Hadrian,* "I have done much rebuilding. To reconstruct is to collaborate with time gone by, penetrating or modifying its spirit, and carrying it toward a longer future. Thus beneath the stones we find the secret of the springs." Will I really have discovered under the stones of Siena the true secret of the spring? Who knows, maybe just in part. In the end, the greatest secret is knowing that in the book of life there are still so many more pages to turn.

DREAMING OF CINEMA

What is it about a cold autumn Monday where a constant rain makes the stones of the center shiny and slippery? The perfect last stop for today is the **cinema Nuovo Pendola** (Via San Quirico 13, 📞 +39 0577 43012). Taking a break in its comfortable seats in front of a heartwarming show is just what we need. We could dream *Sweet Dreams,* maybe of *Wild Strawberries* on *Sunset Boulevard*, or maybe of *A Golden Boy,* or *The Visitor...*

The most observant readers will have caught on to the movie titles "game," but maybe I should reveal the common thread binding them: they are all films shown during the festival entitled **Ciak, si gira: psicoanalisi al cinema** (Action! Psychoanalysis in film). After the end credits, during these autumn Monday nights, a group of psychoanalysts incite reflection amongst the spectators, reaching for their most intimate emotions.

The Pendola is an old-fashioned cinema, such as those that keep older, restored films in their original language. Retro room, vaulted ceiling, dim lights: if you close your eyes you might find yourself in the Latin quarter in Paris, in one of those hidden, "alternative" cinemas behind the Sorbonne with showtimes starting at 10:00 a.m. A D.O.C. cinema? Exactly: a "Denomination of Cinematographic Origin" since 1980. Once you enter, make sure to ask for **Franco Vigni**, movie critic, so you can hear some anecdotes about movies filmed in the Chianti and Val d'Orcia areas. Not many people know that Siena has been the set of numerous productions on the big screen: from Blasetti's *Palio* (1932), to Minghella's *The English Patient* (1996) to Scott's *The Gladiator* (2000). Franco will know which itineraries to follow to search out Siena "in the mirror of cinema", as per the subtitle of his book *Come* *onde del mare*. The Sienese remember the filming of *Quantum of Solace* (Forster, 2008), with James Bond escaping from *Piazza del Campo* while being chased from the rooftops into the *Palazzo Pubblico*, or Michael Bay's 6 *Underground* (2019), when they witnessed a green Alfa Romeo propelled at full speed and special effects that made the car "fly" in the middle of the city.

For those who can never get enough of moving images, there are other cinemas in the city (🔊 www.sienacinema.it): the largest and most modern is the **Metropolitan**, in the gallery off of Piazza Matteotti (known to locals as the Piazza della Posta, where the main post office is located); a bit more cozy is the **cinema Odeon**, near Piazza Tolomei, while the **Alessandro VII** (also called "Cineforum") is in Piazza dell'Abbadia, next to the San Donato church with its 17th century entranceway.

And in the summer? The **Cinema in Fortezza** is one of best ways for both tourists and Sienese alike to spend their evenings. From the end of June to the end of August, the large amphitheater turned outdoor cinema in the Medicean Fortress projects films in collaboration with the Cinema Nuovo Pendola (🔊 www.cinemanuovopendola.it). You can sit in the chairs set up on the ground floor in front of the screen or, and this is what I prefer, with pillows in hand, you can climb the stairs and sit in the amphitheater with the starry sky framing the big screen.

In August many of the surrounding towns in the Siena province participate in the **Visionaria Fuori Fuoco** film festival (🔊 www.visionaria.eu); free independent film screenings in San Gimignano, Castelnuovo Berardenga, Sovicille or Gaiole in Chianti give film enthusiasts a chance to meet and engage with both actors and directors present in the local *piazze*.

But that's not all! The **Terra di Siena Film Festival** (🔊 www.terradisienafilmfestival.eu), at the end of September, is a week of international scope that awards the winning work with the Sanese d'oro, the antique currency of the Republic of Siena. Since 1996 many masters of cinema have brought fame to this festival: Greenaway, Polanski, Bertolucci to name a few, but some can still feel the goosebumps from Emir Kusturica's show in 2001 that delighted spectators with a concert together with his *No Smoking Band*: extraordinary moments in which Piazza del Campo, itself a stunning setting, was transformed into a stage where cinema "danced" to the rhythm of music.

The Great Race

A surprising conversation

- Hey, how's it going? Are you excited?
- *Yeah, just a bit.*
- I noticed. I've been watching you for a while, off by yourself in the back, not really knowing how you got here and what all this commotion around you is.
- *I feel like you just read my mind. How did you know?*
- I'm not psychic, but I've been in your shoes before. I look in your eyes and see the same emotions that I felt the first time I went past that doorway and "tasted" the **tufo**.
- *Did you ever want to run away?*
- No, never. Despite the confusion, I've always trusted everyone around us.
- *You know, when I'm out in the open air it just seems easier. I concentrate on myself and don't pay attention to all those people out there. Here, though, my heart seems to pound so much harder.*
- I know, it's normal. But those are momentary concerns, you'll see. It's the price you pay for your first time. The best way to see if I'm right is to try, put yourself out there, confront that wall of *contradaioli* and emotions on the other side of this courtyard.
- *Eh, you make it seem so easy.*
- I didn't say it was easy. I only said that you can do it. I've seen you around a few times; you're talented, there's no doubt about that. It would be a shame to waste it on fear.

- *Now, wait a minute.... Are you? You're...?*
- Yes, it's me. I'm the one who won last time.
- *It's so good to meet you! Sorry, I was so distracted with my own thoughts that I didn't even recognize you.*
- Don't worry about it, one victory hasn't changed my life. I plan on carrying on for a while.
- *There's so much I want to ask you.*
- Go right ahead. I'm not sure why but I like you, I don't want to be secretive.
- *It's like a dream come true. So, tell me, what happens now?*
- Look around. There's ten of us left in here, the last ten, the best. Soon, when the moment's right, we'll split up. It's the day of the **tratta**. You will hear people jumping for joy when they call out my number and match it to a contrada. Afterwards everyone will go their own way. Don't think you'll be left all alone, that will never happen. Instead, there will be several of them taking care of you. This is the moment that marks the beginning of the four most exciting days of your life. And tonight we will be back together again, right here, ready for our first appearance in front of everyone.
- *Sounds good so far. Then what?*
- Then it really begins. You know the way, I'm sure you've done it several times.
- *Yes, but alone... Here, in this setting, everything seems different.*
- There's still time. Should we go over it again?
- *Well, maybe...*
- So, let's start with the **mossa**, the starting point. Have you seen where the black and white flag is, the **bandierino**?
- *Yes.*
- Good. Next to you is the **verrocchio**, the sort of platform where the **mossiere** stands, the man who gives the start. For now, let's leave him there, with his attentive eye and his foot on the pedal below, ready to release the **canapi**, the ropes. You're inside, between those two taut ropes both in front of and behind you. Don't push on them, stay calm. Find some space and stand your

ground to keep the spot you earned, possibly on the inner side, close to the **steccato**, the fencing. You will need strength and patience. As soon as the last one of us, the **rincorsa**, passes the **verrocchino**, the instrument behind you that keeps the second rope taut, it begins. In that moment spring into action and let yourself go. Putting your head forward right away is fundamental.

- *I'm not worried about that: they told me I'm a starter.*
- Do you think that's enough? After the start it's a free-for-all; a second passes, you pass **Fonte Gaia** and you're already going downhill, trying to keep the right path towards the most difficult curve, **San Martino**, which often decides the race. You'll see some white **mattresses** at the end of that turn: they aren't there for taking a nap, but to protect us if something goes wrong. Once past that curve that lasts as long as a chill running down your spine, run as fast as you can in the straightaway that lines the Palazzo Pubblico: long and reassuring.
- *Oh, finally... and there I can catch my breath, right?*
- Not at all. Because that's the part where you have to prepare for the next curve, a bit slower but maybe more intimidating than the first, where the inexperienced pay dearly.
- *Is it the famous Casato?*
- Bravo, I see you've studied the course!
- *After, though, I can finally slow down a bit...*
- Now is the moment to pick up speed! You have to prove to yourself and others that there's still some strength in you. Be careful, three laps are a lot, and if you've already spent all your energy by this point you're in trouble. You have to learn to ration your energy, to hold back and then let go at the right moment.
- *It's much, much harder than what I thought, that you just needed to run fast.*
- That's the least of your worries here. But don't lose heart. You still have time to refine your strategy. The **prove** are just for that.

- *Does it count at all if you win those?*
- Absolutely not, even though they are of varying importance. The **prova generale**, for example, the evening trial before the fateful day, is always…how can I put it…lively. A lot of people in the piazza, songs, joy, and after the trial race everyone is out to dinner in their *contrada*. And when I say everyone, I mean everyone: thousands and thousands of people on the street, eating and sharing one of the most intense moments, those moments which precede the **carriera**.
- *I can't wait to be a part of that.*
- I'm sorry, friend, you have to go to bed early, even though I'm sure that they'll let you take a peek. Then, as I was telling you, there are the less important trial races, like the **provaccia**, the last trial on the morning of the Palio. More like a stroll than a real race.
- *Then there's the afternoon…*
- Oh yes, that seems to last a week, there's so much going on. It's as if time slows down, every second lasts a minute, every minute an hour, and so on. And as time goes on it starts to accelerate and intensify.
- *I heard that we have to go to church, is that true?*
- Of course. Why? Do you have something against the **benedizione**? The blessing rite? Actually, that's one of the most emotional moments, a wonderful hug with your people and the priest saying your name and then 'Go, and come back a winner.' Be careful, don't let your heart beat too fast, they might hear it.
- *I already feel like I'm living these emotions through your eyes. On one hand I can't wait to savor those moments, on the other I'm not sure if I'm ready.*
- Hey, don't think about it just yet. Even though I told you that day will be intense, at a certain point you'll see there will be time to show off your talents…
- *Me? A show-off? I mean maybe a little…*
- There's nothing to it. During the **historical parade**, dressed up with the **saddlecloth** and **spennacchiera**, the *contrada's* colors

on your forehead, you'll be able to flaunt your beauty. Just for a moment, though; after that you have to think of one thing only: running.
- *After all that we will end up back here, in the **entrone**, the court-yard in Palazzo Pubblico, before the last call, the shot from the **mortaretto**.*
- Exactly. It will be a bit different from the other days. Some seemingly small things may make a big difference. First of all, all the jockeys will have a **nerbo**, or whip.
- *Hmmm.*
- Then, another important thing, the order at the ropes will not be pre-established like during the trial races but will be extracted randomly at the last minute. That order will be written inside of a sealed envelope that, during a surreal silence, will be brought to the *mossiere* by a policeman and, keeping it in sight for everyone to see, the *mossiere* will open it and call out each *contrada* one by one.
- *So, I won't know who I'll be next to until the very end. Or if I'll be the last one!*
- That's the beauty of this great race. Some call it fate, others destiny, even others pure chance. Call it as you wish, but to run in the Palio you have to take it into account. But beside all of this, you should worry about what you do best.
- *Ah... And if my jockey falls?*
- You keep going. This is a **bareback race**, so it's not uncommon to find yourself running alone. And here we can even win **scossi**, without the jockey. The *contrada* wins, not the jockey. And don't worry if someone blocks your way: it could be your **rival**, trying to interfere with your victory.
- *Got it. And then what do I have to do?*
- Do you want to be remembered as one in a million, just another name, a **brenna** as they say in Siena, or do you want to be the new **bombolone?** So don't ask me what you have to do, but run, my son, run carefully and fast. At the end of the day, you're a horse!

PALIO JARGON

Alfiere (Flag-waver): a representative of a *contrada* whose responsibility is that of playing the flag.

Alleata (Ally): Each *contrada* may have *contrada* "friends" or "alliances" with one or more *contrade*.

Bandierino: small iron flag with the *Balzana* (Siena's black and white crest), that marks the start and finish for the race.

Barbaresco: he who, during the days of the Palio, is responsible for taking care of the horse when it's not with the jockey, living symbiotically with it and never leaving it alone.

Barbero: the horse that runs the Palio. It is also the name of wooden marbles, painted with the colors of the seventeen *contrade*, that represent a favorite game of Sienese children.

Benedizione del cavallo (Blessing of the horse): In the churches of the ten *contrade* participating in the race, a priest appointed by the *contrada* blesses the horse and the jockey the afternoon of the race, around 3:00 p.m. for the July Palio, or 2:30 p.m. in August. This is a rare occasion to see a horse welcomed and blessed inside a church.

Bombolone: one of the favorite horses, expected to win.

Brenna: slow horse, not one of those the *contrada* members rejoiced over at the moment of the Tratta.

Canape/canapi: ropes that define the starting point. The *mossiere* lowers them at the moment when the *rincorsa*, or last horse enters into the roped area.

Capitano (Captain): The highest elected member of the *contrada* during the Palio days. This person works with a trusted staff and is responsible for preparations and strategies for obtaining a victory.

Cappotto (lit. **winter coat**): this term is used when a *contrada* wins both the July and August Palios. When this occurs, you may see *contrada* members wearing long winter coats in the summer.

Carriera: the Palio, the races of July 2 and August 16, that consists of 3 laps around Piazza del Campo.

Carroccio: the large cart pulled by oxen that wraps up the Historical Parade and upon which is carried the Palio banner. It represents the pride of the freedom of Siena during the Republic era.

Casato: the uphill curve in the *piazza*, the last one before the finish. The Historical Parade enters the *piazza* from the Casato.

Chiarina: old style of trumpet, with a long body and particular sound. In Siena, the "March of the Palio" accompanied by the sound of these

trumpets announces important moments throughout the Palio days.
Colonnini di piazza: short marble columns that border Piazza del Campo (there are 71 around the "shell" and 19 lined up in front of Palazzo Pubblico.) They were once used as units of measurement to indicate the distance between horses during the race.
Comparsa: the group of representatives for each *contrada* (among which two *alfieri* and one *tamburino*).
Contradaioli: people belonging to one of the seventeen *contrade*.
Dare la mossa: when the last horse reaches the starting point, the *mossiere* lowers the ropes and gives the start of the race to the ten horses.
Drappellone: the painting on a silk banner given to the winning *contrada*, often called the "rag" by the Sienese.
Entrone: the courtyard in the *Palazzo Pubblico*, where the ten horses and jockeys gather before the start of the Palio.
Fazzoletto: (lit. **tissue**) a kerchief particular to each *contrada* that is worn by the *contradaioli* during the days of the Palio (only when the *contrada* is participating), or during certain occasions. It represents a strong sense of belonging and is given to every child at the moment of his or her *contrada* baptism, a laic baptism that ties the person to the *contrada* for life.
Fonte Gaia: monumental fountain in Piazza del Campo.
Gualdrappa: ornamental cloth used for decorating the horse's back during the historical parade.
Masgalano: prize given to the most elegant *Comparsa* from both the July and August Historical Parades (thus the name deriving from the Spanish *más galante*).
Materassi: mattresses fixed in place at the San Martino curve, to soften the blows to horses and jockeys. While they were once wool mattresses, today they use the same advanced protective materials as they do for the Formula One races.
Monta a pelo: bare-back riding.
Mortaretto (o **Mortaletto**): the "cannon" that announces the exit of the ten *contrade* participating in the Palio from the *entrone* to make their way to the starting line. One shot announces the end of a trial race, or, on the day of the Palio, a false start (or a start that the *mossiere* doesn't consider valid). Three shots announce the end of the Palio and thus the official victory of a *Contrada*.
Mossa: place in which the ten *contrade* running the Palio gather for the start of the race. This term is also used for the moment in which

the actual race begins. Traditionally, a *giovane*, or "young" *mossa* is used when the ropes have been lowered by the *mossiere* before the last horse has reached the *verrocchino*, while a *vecchia*, or "old" *mossa* signifies the *mossiere's* late reaction to lowering the ropes, as the last horse has already passed him.

Mossiere: the person responsible for lining up the horses between the ropes of the *mossa* to allow the race to start once the *rincorsa* has entered them. Traditionally, and for safety reasons, he is taken away as soon as the race begins and never watches the unfolding or result of the race.

Nerbo (whip): dried ox tendon used for spurring one's horse, or with which the jockeys can hit each other during the race.

Palchi: wooden and iron bleachers, setup at the outlying limits of the *piazza*, where spectators can watch the race seated.

Passeggiata Storica (o Corteo Storico): the long *Historical Parade* of dressed representatives from the *contrade* that precedes the Palio.

Priore: the elected person who administrates the *contrada* during the year, excluding the days of the Palio, organizing events and managing its various activities.

Prove (trials): the six trial races taking place from the evening of the Tratta and concluding the morning of the Palio, useful for getting horses and jockeys used to the *piazza*.

Provaccia (lit. **bad trial**): the last trial before the race, held on the mornings of July 2 and August 16.

Prova generale: the trial race, literally "rehearsal race," held the evening before the Palio and followed by the famous dinner of the same name in all the *contrade*.

Purga: literally "purge", this term is used when one's rival contrada wins the Palio. This "state of being" is one that no *contrada* member hopes to experience after the race. Ripurgato, re-purged, could be any *contrada* that, even though they had a good horse, in the end didn't win. This term is also used for the *contrada* who comes in second.

Rincorsa: the tenth and last *contrada*, whose horse must enter into the roped area last, thus signaling the start of the race.

Rione: the territory of a *contrada*.

Rivale (o avversaria): some *contrade* have a rival or adversary, a *contrada* that they are not on good terms with. In colloquial terms, it is considered an "enemy."

San Martino: the first curve that the horses come across. It is downhill and protected by padding to soften the blow or eventual fall.

Scosso (lit. **shaken**): the horse that runs without a jokey during the Palio. If the horse ends up coming in first, the victory is still valid, as it can be recognized by the *spennacchiera*, or ribbon on its forehead.

Soppresse: the six "suppressed" *contrade* that do not exist anymore in Siena: *Gallo* (rooster), *Leone* (lion), *Orso* (bear), *Quercia* (oak), *Vipera* (viper) and *Spadaforte* (sword).

Soprallasso: a usually very tame horse the jokey rides during the Historical Parade.

Spennacchiera: ribbon displaying the colors of the *contrada*, placed on the horses' forehead to identify to which *contrada* it belongs.

Steccato: wooden fencing that marks off the track.

Sunto: the name of large bell in the Torre del Mangia. The day of the Palio it acts as a metronome, sounding out the various moments of the day.

Tamburino: he who represents the *contrada* by playing the drum and giving the rhythm to the flag-waving.

Tratta dei cavalli: a series of trial runs (*batterie*), the mornings of June 29 and August 13, used to select the ten horses that will run in the Palio.

Tufo: mix of several types of earth laid down on the track around the *piazza* to make it easier for the horses to gallop.

Verrocchio: a wooden platform where the *mossiere* stands, as well as the pedal used to lower the ropes.

Verrocchino: the device that holds the back rope up.

Zucchino: helmet displaying the colors of the *contrada* used by jockeys to protect their heads during the Palio and trial races.

Which *contrade* run in the Palio?

Ten *contrade* participate in every Palio. Considering that the July and August Palios are separate but equal, the remaining seven from each Palio of a particular year (of the 17 total) run "by right" the next year (if you don't run in July 2023, it will be your "right," or turn, to run in July 2024; those who don't run in August 2023, will run "by right" in August 2024). In order to reach ten, three *contrade* are drawn during the *estrazione delle contrade* and the flags of the three *contrade* extracted are hung from the windows of the Palazzo Pubblico.

THE 17 CONTRADE
(For the emblems, see the inside cover flap)

AQUILA

Symbol:	Eagle, representing combativeness
Colors:	Golden yellow with black and deep blue lines
Motto:	*Dell'Aquila il rostro, l'ugna e l'ala* – "The beak, nail and wing of the Eagle"
Military Companies:	San Pietro in Castelvecchio, Casato di Sopra, Aldobrandino del Mancino
Patron Saint and Feast Day:	Holy Name of Mary, September 12
Allies:	Civetta, Drago
Adversary:	Pantera

www.contradadellaquila.com

BRUCO

Symbol:	Caterpillar, representing industriousness
Colors:	Yellow and green with deep blue border
Motto:	*Come rivoluzion suona il mio nome* – "My name sounds a revolution"
Military Companies:	San Pietro a Ovile di Sotto
Patron Saint and Feast Day:	The Visitation of Mary, first Sunday of July
Allies:	Istrice, Nicchio, Torre
Adversary:	none

www.nobilcontradadelbruco.it

CHIOCCIOLA

Symbol:	Snail, representing prudence
Colors:	Red and yellow with deep blue strips
Motto:	*Con lento passo e grave nel campo a trionfar Chiocciola scende* – "With slow and heavy steps the *Chiocciola* arrives victorious in the *piazza*"
Military Companies:	San Marco, San Quirico, Monistero
Patron Saint and Feast Day:	Holy Apostles Peter and Paul, June 29
Allies:	Istrice, Pantera, Selva
Adversary:	Tartuca

www.contradadellachiocciola.it

CIVETTA

Symbol:	Owl, representing guile
Colors:	Black and red with white strips
Motto:	*Vedo nella notte* – "I see in the night"
Military Companies:	San Vigilio, San Pietro in Banchi, San Cristoforo
Patron Saint and Feast Day:	Saint Anthony of Padua and San Bernardo Tolomei, June 13
Allies:	Aquila, Istrice, Giraffa, Pantera
Adversary:	Leocorno

📶 www.contradadellacivetta.it

DRAGO

Symbol:	Dragon, representing ardour
Colors:	Pink and green with yellow border
Motto:	*Il cor che m'arde divien fiamma in bocca* – "My burning heart becomes a flame in my mouth"
Military Companies:	Sant'Egidio, San Donato ai Montanini
Patron Saint and Feast Day:	Saint Catherine of Siena, last Sunday in May
Ally:	Aquila
Adversary:	none

📶 www.contradadeldrago.it

GIRAFFA

Symbol:	Giraffe, representing elegance
Colors:	Red and White
Motto:	*Altius caput maior gloria* – "Higher capital, greater glory"
Military Companies:	San Pietro a Ovile di Sopra
Patron Saint and Feast Day:	Visitation of Mary, first Sunday in June
Allies:	Civetta, Istrice, Pantera
Adversary:	none

📶 www.contradadellagiraffa.it

ISTRICE

Symbol:	Porcupine, representing sharpness
Colors:	White with red, black and blue arabesque pattern
Motto:	*Sol per difesa io pungo* – "Only in defense I strike"
Military Companies:	Santo Stefano, San Vincenti, la Magione, San Bartolomeo
Patron Saint and Feast Day:	Holy Apostle Bartholomew, August 24
Allies:	Bruco, Chiocciola, Civetta, Giraffa
Adversary:	Lupa

www.istrice.org

LEOCORNO

Symbol:	Unicorn, representing science
Colors:	White and orange with blue border
Motto:	*Fiede e risana al par l'arma c'ho in fronte* – "The weapon I bear on my forehead both harms and heals"
Military Companies:	San Giorgio, Pantaneto, Spadaforte
Patron Saint and Feast Day:	St. John the Baptist, June 24
Allies:	Pantera, Tartuca
Adversary:	Civetta

www.contradaleocorno.it

LUPA

Symbol:	She-wolf, representing loyalty
Colors:	White and black with orange border
Motto:	*Et urbis et senarum signum et decus* – "Crest of Rome, yet the honor of Siena"
Military Companies:	San Donato allato alla chiesa, Sant'Andrea
Patron Saint and Feast Day:	Saint Rocco, August 16 (generally celebrated the first Sunday of September) The *Lupa Contrada* is a sister city with Rome.
Adversary:	Istrice

www.contradadellalupa.it

NICCHIO

Symbol:	Shell, representing discretion
Colors:	Blue with red and yellow
Motto:	*È il rosso del corallo che m'arde in cor* – "The red of the coral burns in my heart"
Military Companies:	Abbadia nuova di Sopra, Abbadia nuova di Sotto
Patron Saint and Feast Day:	Saint Gaetano Thiene, August 7
Allies:	Bruco, Onda, Tartuca
Adversary:	Valdimontone

www.nobilecontradadelnicchio.it

OCA

Symbol:	Goose, representing astuteness
Colors:	White and green with red border
Motto:	*Clangit ad arma* – "Thou shalt sound the call to arms"
Military Companies:	Sant'Antonio, San Pellegrino
Patron Saint and Feast Day:	Saint Catherine of Siena, April 29. The contrada celebrates in May. The *Oca Contrada* is a sister city with Trieste.
Adversary:	Torre

www.contradadelloca.it

ONDA

Symbol:	Dolphin, representing happiness
Colors:	White and Light Blue
Motto:	*Il colore del cielo, la forza del mare* – "The color of the sky, the strength of the sea"
Military Companies:	Casato di Sotto, San Salvadore
Patron Saint and Feast Day:	Visitation of Mary, July 2
Allies:	Nicchio, Tartuca, Valdimontone
Adversary:	Torre

www.contradacapitanadellonda.com

PANTERA

Symbol:	Panther, representing courage
Colors:	Red and blue with white stripes
Motti:	*La Pantera ruggì ed il popolo si scosse / Il mio slancio ogni ostacolo abbatte* – "The Panther roared and the people shook" / "My leap knocks down any obstacle"
Military Companies:	Stalloreggi di Dentro, Stalloreggi di Fuori
Patron Saint and Feast Day:	Saint John the Beheaded, August 29
Allies:	Chiocciola, Civetta, Giraffa, Leocorno
Adversary:	Aquila

www.contradadellapantera.it

SELVA

Symbol:	Forest, representing power
Colors:	Green and Orange with White border
Motto:	*Prima Selvalta in Campo* – "The Selva first in Piazza del Campo"
Military Companies:	Vallepiatta, San Giovanni, Porta Salaia
Patron Saint and Feast Day:	Assumption of the Virgin Mary, August 15, celebrated the fourth Sunday of August
Allies:	Chiocciola, Tartuca
Adversary:	none

www.contradadellaselva.it

TARTUCA

Symbol:	Tortoise, representing tenacity
Colors:	Yellow and Blue
Motto:	*Forza e costanza albergo* – "I house strength and constance"
Military Companies:	Porta all'Arco, Sant'Agata
Patron Saint and Feast Days:	Saint Anthony of Padua, June 13
Allies:	Leocorno, Onda, Nicchio, Selva
Adversary:	Chiocciola

www.tartuca.it

TORRE

Symbol:	Tower supported by an elephant, representing strength
Colors:	Crimson with White and Blue
Motto:	*Oltre la forza, la potenza* – "More than strength, power"
Military Companies:	Salicotto di Sopra, Salicotto di Sotto, Rialto, San Giusto
Patron Saint and Feast Day:	Holy Apostle James and Saint Anne, July 25, celebrated the last Sunday of July.
Ally:	Bruco
Adversary:	Oca

www.contradadellatorre.it

VALDIMONTONE

Symbol:	Ram, representing perseverance
Colors:	Red and yellow with white
Motto:	*Sotto il mio colpo la muraglia crolla* – "The wall collapses under my blow"
Military Companies:	Borgo Santa Maria, Sant'Angelo a Montone, Samoreci (San Maurizio)
Patron Saint and Feast Day:	Madonna of the Good Counsel, celebrated April 26
Ally:	Onda
Adversary:	Nicchio

www.valdimontone.it

Each one of the 17 *contrade* possesses, like a treasure chest, a **museum** within its territory. They are places in which we can find history, art, culture and more. Every museum preserves that invisible thread of memory that ties the past to the present and forms the essence of the *contrada* of today.

Chapter 5 / The Art Lover

Face To Face With Beauty

An Enchanting Dance Among Art

I think of Siena and my mind goes straight to *Stealing Beauty,* one of my favorite Bertolucci films. Carefree, independent, smiling, drea-ming: how I love Liv Tyler, protagonist of this film! In a certain sense I feel close to her, with that healthy yearning to steal beauty that is in all of us. If only I could transform for a second and make the Castle of Brolio in the Chianti region an ideal movie set. "Ready, action" and the "clap" surprises me in the middle of a dance party: everyone quiet, let me dream of that area and that magic. Barefoot, hair in the wind, the swing rhythm going among the grapevines at sunset. I notice the shadow of a man who waits for me under the shade of a centuries-old oak and in the background, in the horizon, the profile of the Torre del Mangia.

This is my Siena: passion, desire, *joie de vivre,* wonders in every cor-ner around me. I hold my breath: let me hold onto this beauty for a moment, although I wish it lasted a lifetime. And then, letting it all out in a long, liberating breath: now I'm ready to tell you about this city, a perpetual summer that welcomes you in its art. Or better, in its countless artistic forms. Those chiseled bells made by hand by the artisans behind the Duomo, on the hill of Via Monna Agnese. Those delicate gazes of the golden women decorating the walls of so many museums in the city. Or maybe it's the antique objects in Piazza del Mercato, that tell of faraway stories. Who did they belong to? Who knows how much they could tell us… and I enjoy picturing myself in the 18th century, brushing my hair with my reflection in a mirror darkened by time.

Siena is art in movement through the centuries, it preserves within itself concrete evidence of a glorious medieval past, that made it famous for its *avantgarde* artists. Now let's go hand in hand, as I want to share with you what I've discovered. Follow me in this enchanted dance and don't worry if you don't know the steps. Just let yourself be guided; let your eyes wander and its beauty will take care of the rest.

The Duomo's floor (*Il Pavimento del Duomo*)
There's no better place to start than at the cathedral, dedicated to the Assumption of the Virgin Mary, that dominates the highest and oldest part of Siena, one of the most renowned examples of Italian **romanesque-gothic cathedrals**. An imposing and precious gem, consecrated in 1179, that preserves within its walls a unique treasure: flooring considered "the greatest, most beautiful and magnificent that has ever been made…" by **Giorgio Vasari**. An immense creation, realized over 500 years in impeccably carved marble, from the 14th to 19th centuries. You'll have to do what I do, choosing to visit during the few months out of the year (usually from June to October) when the flooring is uncovered and displayed in all its grandeur, without the panels that protect it from being worn down over the centuries. Take your time, at least an hour, to "read" all the stories and symbols figured in its 56 carved scenes, many realized by famous Sienese painters and sculptors: Sassetta, Domenico di Bartolo, Matteo di Giovanni and Domenico Beccafumi. Books upon books offer accurate interpretations. I began with that of Marilena Caciorgna, *Virginis Templum. Siena. Cathedral, Crypt, Baptistery*: those pages reveal the most intricate details.

«*Castissimum Virginis Templum Caste Memento Ingredi*» "Remember to enter in the temple of the Virgin in a chaste and pure way," the first frame of the flooring urges, and depicts **Ermete Trismegisto**, "three times the biggest," legendary character of the late Hellenistic period, venerated as a master of knowledge and founder of the current Hermetism philosophy, as he hands over his conscience to the ancient Egyptians.

Then, on the sides, the blocks with the **ten Sibyls**, prophetic virgins from ancient history, realized between 1482-1483, who with grace and elegance announce the arrival of Christ. Returning to the central nave, the main inlays are of the Roman she-wolf (but also that of Siena, as we will see), surrounded by the symbols of other central Italian cities. Further on we see **Pinturicchio**'s *Allegory of the Mount of Wisdom* (1505-1506): you can recognize it by the figure of Fortune, a nude woman holding a wind-blown sail reminding us of Botticelli's *Venus*. If I close my eyes, I can imagine the clinking of the shiny gold jewelry that fall from her basket into the sea; I almost reach out to catch them, that's how real they seem. Look, then, for Matteo di Giovanni's dramatic scene, the *Massacre of the Innocents* (1481): immense, vivid, almost frightening with its seemingly real figures, its fast and ferocious movement. Then, right under the cupola, the 13 inlays composing an immense hexagon with the *Stories of Elijah and Ahab*, partially realized during the 16th century by the Sienese artist Domenico Beccafumi, and later finished in the 19th century by purist painter Alessandro Franchi.

My feet linger in front of the marks that cross and mark the marble, creating volume and space, my gaze taking in the differences. In the first marble inlays, white marble was carved with a chisel and drill, forming ruts that were then filled by black *stucco*: called *graffito* or an inscribed image. Then colored marble was used, cut and pieced together with precision, like a puzzle, creating a pre-established design. This is the technique of the marble artist. A painstaking work that makes the floor of Siena's Duomo a true "composition," in which the discovery of its details and meanings must be done slowly and thoroughly, maybe even with the help of an **audioguide**.

After having admired the view under our dancing feet, we can now look up to the sculptures that embellish the Duomo. To the left of the alter, the magnificent **pulpit by Nicola Pisano** (1268), considered to be a true sculpted **Gospel**, with lions and lionesses holding up the granite columns and the elegant staircase that elevates the grandeur of the structure. Or, heading back towards the entrance, the two chapels on the left nave: that of **St. John the Baptist,** with the bronze statue realized by **Donatello** in 1457, or that of the Piccolomini family chapel, containing four **statues of a young Michelangelo**, dated around 1504. It could be that the proud face of St. Paul is Michelangelo's first self-portrait.

Don't forget to visit the **Libreria Piccolomini**, next to the altar, a collection of lights and colors, beginning from the quasi-hypnotic geometric flooring, passing to the precious decorated manuscripts, leading to the gold-leaf decorated vault with classic "grotesque" motifs. A treasure, more than a library, decorated between 1503 and 1508 by Pinturicchio (who died in Siena and is buried in the church of San Vincenzo, the church of the *Istrice Contrada*) and those in his workshop.

The ten frescoed stories along the walls represent important moments from the life of Pope Pius II, the Sienese Enea Silvio Piccolomini. In the scene dedicated to the *Canonization of Saint Catherine* we can try to find **the portrait of Raffaello** (in red stockings) and **the self-portrait of Pinturicchio** (with a red cap), dressed fashionably for their times. How funny they seem!

As we head towards the exit, this feeling of wonder gives way to the spiritual silence of the **Cappella del Voto** (1660), on the right nave. It's intimate setting is reassuring. Inside a gothic church like the Duomo, in a medieval city like Siena, the baroque masterpieces created by the expert **Gian Lorenzo Bernini** amaze me. In the center the wonderful *Madonna with Child*, known as the Virgin of the Vow by Dietisalvi di Speme (1267). Commissioned to celebrate the victory over the Florentines in the famous Battle of Montaperti (1260), it has always been an object of devotion for the Sienese: who knows how many prayers it has listened to throughout the years, especially during the days of the August Palio, dedicated to the Assumption of the Virgin Mary, when the Palio banner is placed on the high altar and celebrated by the winning *contrada.*

One last thing before leaving the cathedral. You may have noticed that along the central pillars that support the cupola there are **two long wooden shafts** of about 15 meters long each. Let's believe the legend that they were once used to wave the city's banners during the battle of Montaperti. They were so long they could be seen from kilometers away, and thus helped the soldiers orient themselves towards the city. A war relic, celebrating one of the most important historical moments of Siena, the victory against the fierce enemy of Florence, as my intellectual friend will confirm.

The Gate of Heaven (*La Porta del Cielo*)
Now that we've finished our tour inside the Duomo, it's time to experience a new, original point of view. If you're not afraid of heights, let's continue this dance and go through the **Gate of Heaven**, the wondrous guided tour on the rooftops of the cathedral. "This is none other than the house of God; this is the gate of heaven," exclaimed Jacob upon awakening, after having dreamt of a ladder that reached toward Heaven (Genesis, 28:17); thus, the name for this unusual visit. Seventy-nine steps separate us from an unforgettable sight: the first stop is 16 meters up, through a narrow (almost secret) spiral staircase within the right nave's side tower. You can go up in small groups with a special reserved ticket. And it seems we are truly reaching heaven, those blue vaults with golden stars that from the central nave lead your gaze up to the magnificent cupola, with a coffer design, 54 meters high. A true walk of discovery, a walkway below the roof from which we can admire the floor from above and access a "behind the scenes" look of the cathedral through a collection of original tools, materials and instruments used for the construction of the Duomo.

Yet another sight awaits us: narrow walkways lead us outside, to the external colonnade of the cupola, where we can enjoy a magical view of the city, with the Torre del Mangia and Piazza del Campo below us to the left, the *Facciatone* right in front (we'll get to this later) and then, on the right, the bell tower that measures 77 meters, with the octagonal spire protected by four pinnacles. Believe me, from this unusual observation point Siena makes your head spin.

Exiting the cathedral

The time has come to leave. Maybe it's true: it doesn't matter so much how you enter the Duomo of Siena, but rather how you leave it…And after this visit, I have no doubt the magic we experienced will be noticeable to everyone: an invitation to let the beauty and the knowledge of the Duomo inebriate us. As soon as we are past the door, I turn back one last time to observe the outside of the cathedral. The **relief statues** of prophets, Sybils and philosophers that surround the architrave and the gables of the central door seem to be breaking away, with their head poking out, as if they were wanting to whisper something in my ears. At daybreak and sunset on a clear day an almost heavenly light shines on the central rose window, coloring the facade with dreamy pink-orange hues.

The first time I walked up the church's main steps, the statue of the she-wolf nursing two twins (*Romulus* and *Remus*) caught my attention. For a moment I thought that it could have been an homage to Rome, but then I let my intuition guide me and I discovered that it is also the symbol of Siena. The **she-wolf of Siena** is slightly different from her Roman "sister": her head isn't lowered towards the twins, but looking forward. In this specific case she seems to gesture to visitors that it's time to look towards a new revelation: right in front of the cathedral, in fact, is the **Santa Maria della Scala Museum Complex.**

Maestà, Duccio di Buoninsegna, Museo OPA Opera della Metropolitana
© Studio Fotografico Lensini

La Porta del Cielo (The Gate of Heaven)
© Studio Fotografico Lensini (*Virginis Templum*, Sillabe 2013)

Top: *The Palio in Piazza del Campo*
© Paolo Lazzeroni

Right: *Alley in Siena*
© Luciano Valentini

Top: *View of Siena from the Sienese Countryside*
© Giulia Brogi (*Siena. Le stagioni del Palio*, Il Leccio 2013)

Right: *Barbaresco Caring for a Horse*
© Carlo Vigni (*Palio*, Protagon Editore 2009)

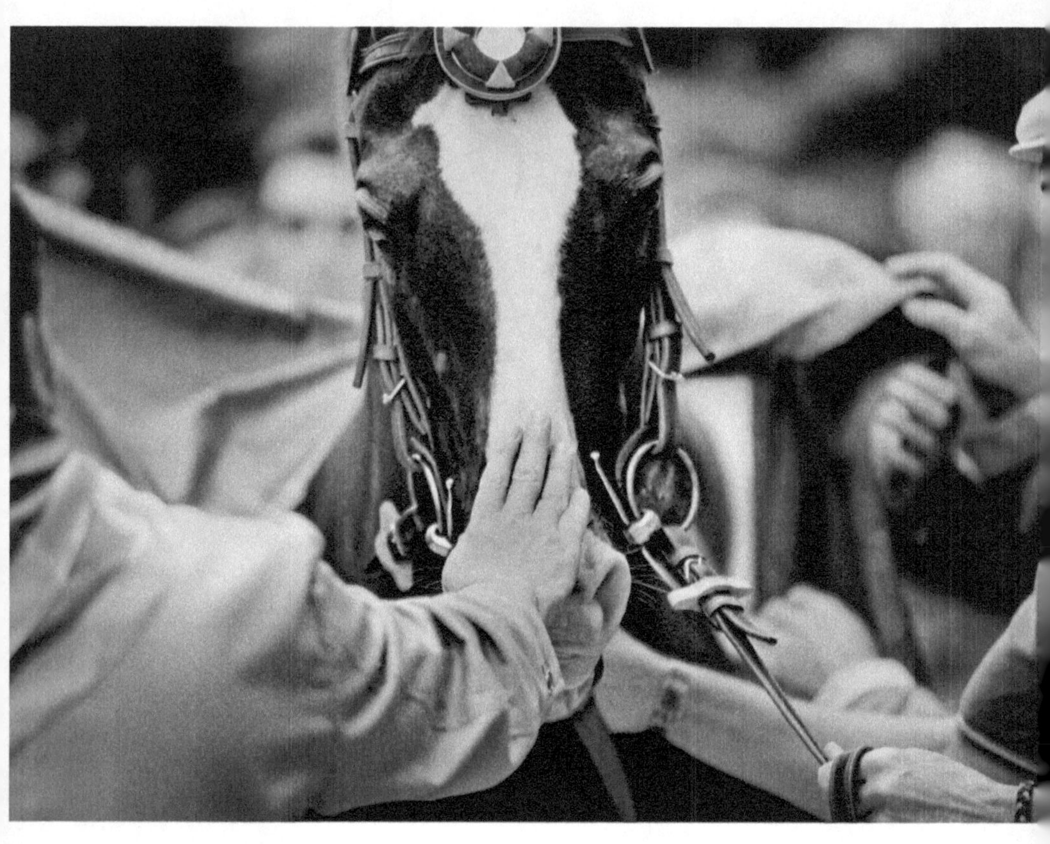

The Blessing of the Horse before the Palio
© Carlo Vigni (*Palio*, Protagon Editore 2009)

Palio, the Night Trials
© Giulia Brogi

Duomo di Siena, View of the Central Nave
© Studio Fotografico Lensini

THE MAGIC SQUARE

Around the corner, on the left side of the cathedral in front of the Bishop's residence, the **magical Sator square** awakens my curiosity, an inscription that may be tied to the Templar Knights. The writing is a Latin palindrome, five words that, read left to right, from top to bottom (and vice versa), indicate the same phrase: **SATOR AREPO TENET OPERA ROTAS**. This enigma has filled pages and pages of books: I've read many, but let's try to find an interpretation that works for us. The simplest and most rudimentary considers "AREPO" as a proper name, and thus the meaning: "Arepo, farmer or sower (SATOR), keeps (TENET) with care (OPERA) the cart's wheels (ROTAS)." Retracing it on religious Christian documents in all of Europe, for many the reference to the sower is an allusion to the Gospel text: "God takes care of his Creations, as man takes care of his fields." But also "God manages and judges the entire Universe." Whatever its true meaning (is it a dedication to a finished work? A Christological symbol? An obscure reference?) I let my thoughts linger on this mysterious puzzle as I search out yet other inscriptions on the white marble. I find more, for example the Latin verse that indicates the tomb of "Master Giovanni who was son of Master Nicola." This one is less difficult to interpret, because the reference brings us to the headstone of **Giovanni Pisano**'s tomb, chief architect of the Opera of the Duomo from May 1284. Legend has it that the sculptor of most of the facade had wanted to be buried right at the foot of his works and this slab testifies as much.

Santa Maria della Scala Museum Complex

Sometimes art "saves" lives: never has a proverb been as accurate as this for the "Santa Maria" (as the Sienese call it), that up through the mid-90's was still the old hospital of Siena. "Della Scala" (of the ladder or stairs) is due to the fact that it is right in front of the stairs to the Duomo, dedicated rightly to St. Mary. On one side of the square is the cathedral, place of faith; on the other, place of charity, where pilgrims passing through the city along the Via Francigena were welcomed.

Among the oldest of Europe (12th century), the Santa Maria della Scala hospital was originally established as a hospice by religious members of the cathedral (even though legend has it that it was founded by a cobbler, a certain beatified Sorore), then becoming a center for assistance for both the sick and abandoned orphans. I like to wander around its immense rooms (more than 15,000 sq. meters, 160,000 sq. ft.), through underground halls, splendidly frescoed rooms, tunnels carved in the sandstone and brick galleries. You can really lose yourself among archeologic finds, treasures and paintings. Luckily the two permanent sections help me to re-orient myself in this mysterious labyrinth on multiple floors: one dedicated to **the origins of Siena** and the other to **Fonte Gaia**. The original marble slabs of that renowned fountain that Jacopo della Quercia sculpted for Piazza del Campo are preserved here, in one of the underground floors of the museum, which is accessed by a staircase and across a courtyard with a cistern (called "Corticella"), a common intersection and reference point for tours.

But what must we stop and see? First and foremost, on the ground floor, the **Sala del Pellegrinaio**, one of the most representative examples of 15th century Sienese painting. When I think that for years it was a hospital room for recovered patients I get goosebumps. Imagine what it would be like to be treated under these vaults and wake up reassured by frescoes painted by Vecchietta, Domenico di Bartolo or Priamo della Quercia. The history of the Santa Maria is illustrated in these images, in a cycle that brings to life the old hospital: we can observe it in the work of the stretcher-bearers, or the nurses' visits; even in the distribution of charity, or the taking in of the "foundlings," abandoned children who were cared for and assisted until adulthood and marriage. I enjoy looking for certain details and expressions: sort of like looking at an album of old photographs.

A beautiful medieval cross section leads into one of the adjacent rooms, the **Old Sacristy**, entirely frescoed by Vecchietta depicting subjects from both the Old and New Testaments. The air is magical here: we can admire the *Madonna del Manto* by Domenico di Bartolo (1444), added at the beginning of the 17th century in a marble-canopied tabernacle, next to the relative "sinopite" (drawn draft found under the frescoed wall). Works of pure talent, within a sacristy known as the **Cappella del Sacro Chiodo**. It contains, in fact, a venerated relic, a holy and whole nail used during the Crucifixion of Christ. Then, displayed in cases are goblets, busts of saints and medals. It is a treasure comparable to the Gospel of Constantinople, with magnificent golden silver binding, decorated with *cloisonné*. On one end of the sacristy is a large credenza destined to preserve these relics, a Reliquary, whose door, painted on both sides by Vecchietta, gives off a colorful, yet timeless appeal.

In the next room, the **Church of the Hospital**, dedicated to the **Most Holy Annunciation** deserves a "devoted" visit. Look up right away: the painted coffer ceiling is the first surprise. Then, in the back, is the immense fresco in the niche in the apse, *Piscina probatica* by Sebastiano Conca, that amplifies the illusion of perspective and depth thanks to the geometry of the painted columns. In the middle of the scene, on the high altar in a play of lights, you won't miss the Christ Risen, sculpted by Vecchietta (1476).

Another collection to admire is the **Piccolomini Spannocchi Collection**, a collection of works donated to the city from this well-known Sienese family. Not only are there works from important northern Italian artists, but also Flemish, German and Dutch. Only have time for two? You don't want to miss **Lorenzo Lotto**, notable Venetian Renaissance artist, with the soft lines and sweet atmosphere of his Nativity, or the genius of **Albrecht Dürer** and the thoughtful humanity of his *San Girolamo*.

The Santa Maria is one of Siena's hidden gems, its **National Archeological Museum** (with rare pieces from Etruscan and Roman times, donated by noble families' private collections from all over the province) and the **Oratorio di Santa Caterina della Notte**, with its unique golden triptych, the *Virgin with Child and Saints* (1400) by Taddeo di Bartolo need no introduction. A true labyrinth of underground tunnels that lead through what were once a medieval barn, cemetery, 17th century wash house, all ending in the fascinating **"internal street."**

Modern technology can help us imagine life in the Santa Maria. Suggestive videos projected on the vaults reveal some of the hospital's secrets: a kind of time machine that immerses us in the wards' hallways (the Sala del Pellegrinaio was once Orthopedia) and uncovers the geological layers as well as its system of internal courtyards. There truly is so much to discover in this immense museum! We try to gather our ideas and take in as much of the history of its secular walls as we leave it behind us and head back into Piazza Duomo.

The OPA Museum

The natural path of the museum complex of the Duomo leads to Piazza Jacopo della Quercia, location of the OPA Museum: **Opera della Metropolitana**. This name refers to the Duomo's workshop, or "factory", an entity created for the supervision of the building and maintenance of the Duomo. Today, the OPA does much more than just preserve its artifacts, it also displays many of Siena's masterpieces.

Of highest importance: the **Sala delle Statue** and the **Sala di Duccio**. The first is a profoundly spiritual room, with its warm lights illuminating Sybils, Prophets and Philosophers of Antiquity, marble statues sculpted by Giovanni Pisano for the facade of the Duomo. You can't help but look down: a hypnotic play of lights and colors emanating from the **original stained glass of the Duomo** captures your gaze. "*Finestra rotonda magna que est post altare beate Virginis Marie Majoris Ecclesie*" – "Large round window placed behind the altar of the Church of the Holy Virgin Mary", states a document from 1287 that attests the realization of the cathedral's rose window.

The stained-glass is an impressive beauty: the chromatic design unfolds across 30 square meters of its six meter diameter. The plates of glass were designed by Duccio di Buoninsegna using a refined technique called *grisaille* (a painting technique used for defining details and undertones, carried out on the internal side of glass), picturing the burial, assumption and incarnation of the Virgin Mary, as well as the Evangelists and Patron Saints of Siena. Its colors emanate a unique visual strength: the golden yellow, pink, ruby red, purple and emerald green emerge from the deep blue background.

After being "dazzled" by this sight, there's still time to dedicate to Donatello's *Madonna of Forgiveness* and Jacopo della Quercia's bas-relief *Madonna and Child, St Anthony the Abbot and Cardinal Antonio Casini*. We reluctantly leave the first room of the museum by taking two ramps of stairs up to the first floor, to the **Sala di Duccio**. On the back wall: **Duccio di Buoninsenga's Maestà**, originally placed on the high altar in the cathedral on June 9, 1311. There are no words to describe it. Even by observing it closely, there will never be enough time to fully appreciate its details. The dim lights in this room invite us to contemplate the work in a religious silence, so that the gold will remain engraved in our minds, together with those solemn faces. This great work was painted on both sides, around the central scene (Virgin Mary on the throne with Jesus as a child on her knees, surrounded by angels and saints) the other "pieces" that form their enormous altarpiece envelop us on all sides of the room with the stories of the *Passion of Christ*. Before leaving the *Sala di Duccio*, we notice the particular signature on the base of the throne: "*O Santa Madre di Dio, sii causa di pace a Siena, sii vita per Duccio perché ti ha dipinta così*" – "Oh, Holy Mother of God, be cause of peace in Siena, be life for Duccio because he painted thee as such." We give ourselves just enough time to "compare" the *Maestà* with another of Duccio's works, the *Madonna with Child* (also known as the *Madonna of Crevole*). As we leave the room we encounter a third masterpiece, the *Birth of the Virgin* by Pietro Lorenzetti (1342), a work that breaks the traditional scheme of triptychs, rendering it dynamic and alive, while at the same time painting its solemnness.

The treasures of the OPA Museum are endless, but I must briefly mention a few: the delicate *Golden Rose* by Bernini and the *Madonna of the Large Eyes* attributed to Maestro di Tressa (8th century), known also for its "historic value." The eve before the Battle of Montaperti, they say the painting was placed on the high altar and prayed to by the entire city, offering her the keys to the city in exchange for victory.

So that we don't fall victim to Stendhal Syndrome, what we need is some fresh air: we follow the flow of visitors through the last rooms, towards the exit. Now, rubbing our eyes from disbelief, we find ourselves on the marvelous panoramic **Facciatone**, the external "frame" from which we can admire the entire city from above. Piazza del Campo is right below us, surrounded by the city's rooftops. We see the Sienese countryside all around us, as it reaches the valleys of Arezzo and the peaks of Mt. Amiata.

The *Facciatone* should have been the facade of the "New Duomo:" a project that began in 1339 aiming to transform the actual central nave into the lateral transept of the new cathedral, becoming its "short" arm. Just think of what a massive construction it would have become. We also learn that the OPA Museum is none other than the space created by the closure of three parts of the right nave of the New Duomo. We can see what is left standing of the original design: the incomplete facade, with two large central windows and an imposing side door, the base for what is now the most suggestive "view" of the city.

The Crypt and the Baptistery

Leaving the OPA Museum to the right, we cross under the beautiful arch by Giovanni d'Agostino. Before taking the stairs ("of Saint Catherine," as the Sienese say), in the left corner a "secret" entrance leads us to the **Crypt**. Discovered only in 1999, it is one of the greatest archeological finds in Siena.

A frescoed room from the second half of the 13th century welcomes us: stories of the Passion of Christ (the *Crucifixion, Taking Christ down from the Cross* and his *Deposition in the Sepulchre*), three masterpieces that amaze onlookers for the lively colors of the drape work and of the figures on a magnificent blue background. Frescoes that seem to penetrate the surrounding walled structure, with its columns, pilasters and decorated geometric and floral-patterned capitals. We are directly under the chorus of the cathedral, where there may have been a lower church connected by a stairway where pilgrims stopped while passing through on the Via Francigena.

As soon as we exit the Crypt, a steep marble staircase leads us directly to the Baptistery. If you're not tired yet, you must stop in the **San Giovanni Battista** Church, known as the **Baptistery**, constructed just below the cathedral. Right in front of us is the **Baptismal Font**: a hexagonal basin with bronze reliefs that serve as a base for a tabernacle, topped by the statue of San Giovanni, seated on a pedestal on its cupola. This is one of the most exemplary sculptures from the 15th century, result of the talent of three of the most important artists of that time: Donatello, Jacopo della Quercia and Lorenzo Ghiberti.

Everything surrounding the Baptismal Font deserves our attention: the apse and the rib vaults are the relief works of one of the masters of 15th century painting, Vecchietta. In the 24 "veils" that make up the sky, the fresco technique is refined with metallic foil, highlighting the play on light. Light spirals that flower from above: if we are careful observers, as we were in the Crypt, we can find some traces of the Duomo, especially near the figure of the Assumption of Mary, a small opening that gives us a "glimmer" of hope, of "ascending" into the cathedral, a tunnel that brings us right into the temple dedicated to the Virgin Mary.

The Pinacoteca Nazionale

In **Via San Pietro**, 200 meters from the cathedral, we run across an elegant facade, decorated by double-arched windows and Guelph merlons: it's that of two historical buildings - Buonsignori and Brigidi - that since 1932 are home to the **Pinacoteca Nazionale**, a national art museum. We don't waste any time and enter the building together. We know that inside its walls we can find some of the greatest Sienese paintings collected by the abbots Giuseppe Ciaccheri and Luigi de Angelis between the end of the 18th century and the beginning of the 19th century, then scientifically organized by Cesare Brandi during the 20th century.

After passing the inner courtyard we go up two floors: the chronological order of the museum begins counterclockwise from the second floor. From this point on, it will be like reading an art history manual, with the numbering of the rooms sounding out the passage of time: from the beginning through the 18th century.

We dance through Sienese art history, its **golden backgrounds** and **polyptychs** on the second floor make our head spin like a pirouette. Let's begin with the elegant *Madonna of the Franciscans* by Duccio and the *Madonna of Mercy* by Simone Martini, with her dark cloak open to take in and protect those who pray to her. We could then get lost in the gazes of the *Annunciation* by Ambrogio Lorenzetti, or in the details of his brother Pietro's monumental *Carmelite altarpiece*. Quickly moving towards the 15th century, we are surrounded by Sano di Pietro, Giovanni di Paolo, Sassetta, Matteo di Giovanni and Vecchietta. There is, however, an unexpected treat: the Mystic *Marriage of St Catherine of Alexandria* by the Lombard painter Michelino da Besozzo, that beautifully captures this ethereal event.

On the first floor, in Room 23, we stop again to admire Pinturicchio's *Holy Family and Young St. John the Baptist*, a tondo that enchants the spectator with the details in the landscape surrounding the protagonists. The Manneristic figurative language of the 16th century comes out best in the works of Domenico Beccafumi and Giovanni Antonio Bazzi (also knows as Sodoma). Let's confront the respective versions of *Christ in Limbo*, set close to one another. Honestly, I prefer the fresco by Sodoma, for its delicate colors and reassuring and balanced expressions, like a "bridge" to Raffaello's works. Turning next to the Beccafumi, who fascinates us with the immense altarpieces (*Fall of the Rebel Angels* is one of his masterpieces) and the enormous paper drafts for the marble artists working on the Duomo pavement, built to scale, and filling an entire room of the museum.

Some last-minute advice? Before leaving, don't forget the magnificent view from Room 26: its windows offer a beautiful panorama on the houses and valleys below, framed by the **Torre del Mangia** and the cathedral.

Palazzo Pubblico and its Museo Civico

Breathtaking. No other words can describe the two main rooms of the Palazzo Pubblico of Siena: the *Sala del Mappamondo* and *Sala dei Nove*, now part of the Museo Civico. Few cities in the world can compare. We are in Piazza del Campo, heading through the Cortile del Podestà, the courtyard right below the famous Torre del Mangia. After climbing two flights of stairs, the next two hours will be spent enraptured by its medieval gothic atmosphere.

The **Palazzo Pubblico** was built in just over ten years, between the end of the 13th century and beginning of the 14th, to house the nine governors of the Republic of Siena (the Government of Nine). It's considered one of the main civic buildings of Italy and its rooms are a trip through the history of the city. It is said that all of Siena's fates have been decided in these rooms, that today contain extraordinary works of art.

We continue our visit in this order: on the first floor, after the bookshop we walk into the **Sala del Risorgimento (Italian Unification)**, recognizable by its walls recounting the story of Vittorio Emanuele II, first king of united Italy. Right after, the **Sala di Balìa** with its late gothic frescoes, where the executive branch of the government met, (the once Balia magistrate). Continuing straight, we end up in the **Sala del Concistoro**, memorable for its concave ceiling entirely frescoed by Beccafumi.

With light steps and almost holding our breath, we are shaking from excitement as we are about to enter the **Sala del Mappamondo (Room of the World Map)**, where the Republic Counsel would meet. First, though, we stop right in front of the **Cappella dei Signori (Chapel of the Lords)**: our attention falls immediately on the splendid wrought iron gate (designed by Jacopo della Quercia); and then, on the two sides of the altar, the wooden inlaid seats of the choir, sculpted by Domenico di Niccolò (dei Cori) between 1415 and 1428.

Now we finally enter the large room that we've been waiting for and look to our left: surprise and goosebumps are the first words that come to mind when I think of my first "encounter" with **Simone Mar-**

tini's *Maestà*. The first sight of it leaves me speechless: the whole wall, about 10 meters long, is entirely covered by one of the most admirable masterpieces of all of European gothic painting (completed in 1315, with a second intervention in 1321). A less ethereal Maestà than Duccio's, more realistic, conveying an intrinsic moral and civic message (it was commissioned by the Government of the Nine so that the Virgin would watch over the city). In Duccio's, the gold background and the human figures created an aesthetically byzantine and fixed solemnity. Here, instead, the ample portions of blue sky, the depth created by the canopy and its curtains (adopted by Giotto), the chromatic range and the expressivity of the faces transform the scene into a sort of "court;" and the Madonna becomes more "human," so much so to seem a queen among knights and ladies.

We give ourselves as much time as possible to contemplate this masterpiece: getting just a few centimeters from the wall and lifting our eyes towards the ceiling. From this close, and with our low perspective, this multi-material show above us is blinding. Those are real golden leaves applied to the halos on the wall, pieces of glass glimmering on the throne, the gem on the Virgin's clothing is a real crystal, just as the parchment in the hand of the baby Jesus.

Now we turn to observe the opposite wall and discover why this room is called the Sala del Mappamondo (Room of the World Map). The name derives from a large **Map** that represented Siena at the middle, and all around, its conquered territories: a circular disk painted by Ambrogio Lorenzetti (1344), gone. On the frescoed wall we can see just some traces of it, with some scratch marks and a noticeable hole where the pivot stood and around which the "disk" turned.

Just above, we notice the figure of a knight suspended between reality and fantasy, riding a horse on two legs: he's the famous *Guidoriccio da Fogliano* by Simone Martini (1328). The scene tells of the *Siege of the Castle of Montemassi*; among the Maremma hills the castle is recognizable and, far off, the Sienese encampment. If you look close enough, the details of the design on the horse's saddlecloth is made with motifs in relief obtained by the use of a particular technique called "punching."

And now, the **Sala dei Nove (Room of the Nine)**, with its magnificent fresco across three walls, the *Allegories of Good and Bad Government* by Ambrogio Lorenzetti (1338-1340). Here represented are the ideals that would have guided the Nine in the administration of the city: a perfectly realized technique of self-celebration and political "propaganda" through the most effective medium of the times, painting. This cycle of paintings embraces us and seems to immerse us in the middle of a large mirror: on one side the city lives in peace and serenity because supported by a Good government; on the other, a symmetric, specular world, but as if under the effect of a distorted lens. A world in ruin and depravation, with a corrupt administration at the root. In the middle, between the two walls, the Common Good (the City of Siena) is the figure of the old man with the black and white cloak (the colors of the Balzana) and with the she-wolf at his feet as it nurses the twins (emblem of the city), accompanied by the virtues: Peace, Strength, Prudence, Magnanimity, Temperance, Justice, seated under Faith, Hope and Charity.

It's not difficult to grasp the sense of the allegory: where Justice (the female figure with the scale) is assisted by Hope, Siena can live in Harmony and Safety (the angelic woman flying over the walls of the city). Every character tells a story that lets us dream and "breathe in" medieval sounds and aromas: from the bride in a red dress on the white horse to the group of dancing women; from the teacher in a school to the shepherd with his flock. A utopian city where order prevails, where all the shops are open, the animals grazing freely and even in the countryside goods and people travel safely among the cultivated hills.

A terribly different story is "reflected" on the opposite wall, in which Tyranny (the cross-eyed, devil-like being) has Vices as his counsel, while Justice is in chains. This is the *Allegory of the Effects of Bad Government,* that bring death and destruction to the city, military on the street, shops closed and where Fear (dark demon-like figure) hovers over the countryside. It's our job to choose a side...

Now, before leaving the Museo Civico, don't be discouraged by the 51 stairs leading up a steep ramp that you come across during your visit. They lead directly to "paradise:" a monumental 14th century *loggia*, known as the **Loggia dei Nove (Loggia of the Nine)**, that offers a magnificent view on Piazza del Mercato and the whole valley to the south, towards the Val d'Orcia. Here the nine governors of the Republic came to get some fresh air, as it was forbidden for them to leave the building in the two months of their term.

If, leaving the building, you should notice a temporary exhibit being held in the underground areas below the building, be bold! Descend into the **Magazzini del Sale (Salt Warehouse)**, old cisterns and storage area, today fascinating exposition rooms, where, among brick vaults and wide rooms you can find the ideal location for shows usually dedicated to contemporary art.

And so – what a shame! – this enchanting trip is coming to an end. Let's go back to my first image of Siena in *Stealing Beauty*. Do you remember? Yes, after this kaleidoscope of art and wonder, I think that the city knows just how to accompany our solitary dance. Slow, passionate, free, magical. Just like Bertolucci's Liv Tyler, try to wander around with a proud gaze and hair in the wind: the whole historical center of Siena is a **UNESCO World Heritage Site** and I'm sure that it won't be difficult to run into, here and there, in the narrowest streets or in the hidden churches, unexpected and striking flashes of beauty.

Chapter 6 / The Foodie

Appetite Comes While... Wandering

For those "hungry" for Siena 365 days a year

"Everyone eats and drinks, but few appreciate taste," my inseparable notebook reminds me. Between a sauce stain and a big oil spot, Confucius' famous aphorism is among the first few lines and accompanies me every day, almost like a warning to not just fill my stomach to satiate my hunger, but to let myself be seduced and inebriated by flavors. And you? Are you like those travelers, like me, that in every place you've "tasted" you love to slip into the most hidden taverns to eat elbow to elbow with the locals and steal secrets from their menus?

Good. If you want to follow me in this path of discovery of the culinary side of Siena, you will first have to show me you're up for the adventure! Here's a quick test: do you know the Chinese culinary culture of "tasteless food?" Never heard of it? No way, black apron for you! It's the ideology that supports "neutrality" as a potential for all flavors and origin of every possibility. This last question can save you: do you follow current trends both in the kitchen and at the table by looking for the bland and light? Ok, I see you shaking your head from left to right…maybe there's a reason for this. As good foodies let's be clear, we are always searching for new flavors. Like truffle dogs, we can smell out the "goodness" in dishes.

Perfect. You've convinced me. Tie that napkin around your neck and arm yourself with fork and knife: let's begin a tasty meal that's going to last an entire chapter. Yes, because you have to know that in the Sienese culinary dictionary "light" and "bland" are not on the

menu. Just think that a "very light" Sienese tripe dish could be served mid-morning in the middle of the summer.

Among the many *contrada* traditions, there is one, in fact, that embraces the very un-dietetic spirit of the Palio City: called **Trippa in Società (Tripe in *Contrada*)**, a regular event held in almost all the *contrade*.

How does it work? It occurs twice a year during Palio preparations, June 29 and August 13 to be precise, during the days of the *Tratta*, (the choosing of the horses that will run the Palio and assigning of them to the ten participating *contrade*). It's an inaugural moment of Palio festivities, lasting four intense days. That morning (after 10 a.m.), *contrada* members meet up in their respective *contrade* for "breakfast" after the *batterie*, the trials ran in Piazza del Campo around 8:30 a.m. Could eating tripe at this strange time be a way to exorcise the fear of getting stuck with an awful horse? Or maybe they fill their stomachs in order to unburden their minds?

Per tradition this is a propitiatory ritual aimed at attracting good fortune (in Siena, when you hear talk of *Kabbalah*, you should think of a series of superstitious practices carried out during the most important moments of the Palio). Get invited by a "native" friend: the *trippa alla senese* is cooked in a delicious, spicy tomato sauce, and sharing a table with some *contradaioli* (*contrada* members) is a once in a lifetime experience! If you bring them luck (and "your" *contrada* ends up winning), you'll be a special guest for life!

Palios aside, Siena is also "delicious" during the rest of the year: on cold winter days *ricciarelli, copate, cavallucci* and *panforte* will not only give you a sugar rush, but put a smile on your face. They are traditional Sienese sweets you won't want to miss, containing almonds, walnuts, orange peel or candied fruits in different amounts. *Ricciarelli* are quite well known as they are the envy of all of Italy (today they are labeled IGP – Indication of Geographic Protection). These soft cookies made of almond flour and enriched with egg white, sugar, candied orange peel, are then covered in an inviting layer of powdered sugar. Many say their name derives from the curled shape of an antique shoe, imported during the Crusades by Ricciardetto della Gherardesca.

Panforte is another renowned dessert that dates back to Medieval times, when it was baked by apothecaries for consumption by noble families and clergy. Today it is a typical Christmas dessert containing almonds, chocolate, candied fruits, a mix of spices (pepper first and foremost) which is the reason for its second name, *panpepato* (literally peppered bread). For it to be considered *truly* Sienese, *panforte* must contain 17 ingredients, as many as the city's *contrade*, so as not to risk leaving out anyone. During the holidays you may also be offered *copate*, a crunchy honey, almond and walnut mix sandwiched by two round, white wafers.

The lesser known *cavallucci* - even though they date back to the Renaissance (common during Lorenzo the Magnificent's time) - rustic cookies, with their lumpy shape, are born from a mix of flour, anice and cinnamon, then flavored with walnuts, the true protagonists of this dessert.

Especially close to November 1, the star of Siena is *pan co' santi* (bread with saints, in honor of All Saints Day), another dessert containing raisins, pepper and walnuts. Many Sienese even eat it for breakfast, starting the day with a stockpile of calories. Others prefer to dip it in wine (best with new, recently bottled wine). Then there's *castagnaccio*, a dessert made with chestnut flour, raisins, pine nuts and rosemary, a traditional product whose origins go back to the 16th century. We recommend you try the one made with chestnuts from the *Monte Amiata IGP*, a special and flavorful kind. Just like cantucci (or *cantuccini*, dry almond cookies, another culinary gem), even castagnaccio is accompanied perfectly with dessert wines, such as *vin santo* from the Sienese hills, or a delicious *Moscadello di Montalcino*.

A true celebration of desserts takes place in **Via Pian dei Mantellini** for **Santa Lucia** (December 13), a traditional festival that smells of childhood memories. You'll find this area filled with typical Sienese sweets stands, as well as those of some "foreign guests": *brigidini* (crunchy disks flavored with anice, typical of Lamporecchio, near

Pistoia) and the *addormenta-suocere* (literally "making your mother-in-law fall asleep" – caramelized almonds or hazelnuts, typical of Umbria and Tuscany). On why they make mother-in-laws fall asleep, think back again to Sienese cuisine and its lack of "lightness."

During February and March, in occasion of the **Festa di San Giuseppe** (March 19 - St. Joseph Feast Day, also celebrated as Father's day in Italy), I recommend you taste the exquisite *frittelle* (also called *giuseppine*), small balls of rice, milk and flour fried in oil and sprinkled with sugar. In Siena the art of the *frittelle* maker is a true talent, so much so that only two families possess the "true" recipe that has been passed down from generation to generation: it won't be difficult to find them among the city's streets.

During Easter time you won't want to miss taking a bite out of the typical *schiacciata di Pasqua* (Easter bread). Soft, high, similar to a *panettone, schiacciata* literally means smashed, and has this name because seven eggs are broken or "smashed" per 1.5kg of flour; because of the amount of eggs the process is long and elaborate. The ingredients are genuine, try to figure them out....with what clues? You will find notes of anice and mint, aromas that pair well with a glass of sweet wine or the ever-important chocolate egg.

After a feast like this, it wouldn't be a bad idea to burn some calories with a nice walk around town, even if we have to keep this book that smells of Siena under our arm, useful for mentally reviewing the secrets of the local cuisine: it's the *Ricettario di Siena*, a recipe book that proposes local classics such as *crostini con la milza* (bread with spleen patè), *fette di pane al cavolo nero* (bread slices with kale), *malfatti* (hand-cut pasta), *zuppa di fagioli* (bean soup), *acciughe sotto pesto* (anchovies in pesto sauce), *scaloppine alla senese* (Sienese veal scaloppine), *ricciarelli* (almond cookies) and *pinolata* (cake with pine-nuts).

Moving towards the warmer seasons, *panzanella* and *pappa al pomodoro* take the front seat. They are dishes originating from the poor farming tradition that use day-old bread and tomato as the main ingredients. The *zuppa di fagioli* (bean soup) or *zuppa di pane* (bread soup), however, is always in season: in Siena this soup is re-boiled the next day, giving the name to the Florentine sister dish, *ribollita*. In local taverns you can find it all year round and at any time of day, including summer. The *zuppa di fagioli* uses day-old bread as well as beans and vegetables (mostly kale), and its flavor remains, if it doesn't get better, when it's heated more than once. A local celebrity, **Lella Cesari Ciampoli**, can illustrate this to us with her profound knowledge of Tuscan and medieval cuisine.

At her **Scuola di Cucina (Cooking School)** at the bottom of the Fontebranda hill, Lella welcomes guests, diners and anyone curious about experimenting the best recipes hands-on. Highly requested by TV, although she has never accepted, Lady Diana's chef and some of Bill Clinton's staff studied with her. "The secret to my soup? First of all, high quality beans that, after soaking for several hours, are cooked very slowly, with no salt. Then I sauté red onions and add in this order: carrot, kale, and half of the beans, pureed. But the true secret is…patience for the slow cooking, without rushing it and paying close attention to not letting it stick. When you taste it, you have to "savor" the flavors of all the ingredients that you used!"

In order to satiate our gastronomic curiosity, we ask Lella how we can associate the four "qualities" of taste to other Sienese dishes. As she once revealed over dinner, Siena "has the *bitter* aroma of chocolate tagliatelle with wild boar sauce, a *sweet* flavor of almond flour and candied fruits. It is *salty* like Tuscan prosciutto that, make sure, must have slightly pink fat. And it drowns, at last, in the *acidity* of tomato sauce, used for a good *pappa al pomodoro*."

Now we're on to **meat** and **Tuscan cold cuts**, other classics that never disappoint in the restaurants: you must absolutely taste the *chianina* (one of the most select red meats) and then unleash yourself on the trays of cuts of *cinta senese*, in its full array from lard to *rigatino* (Tuscan bacon), from *guanciale* (pork cheek) to *prosciutto*, from fine *salame* to *capocollo* (pork shoulder). Don't let their bizarre names scare you, like *soppressata*, *finocchiona* and *buristo*: they may sound intimidating, but won't be to your palate!

Like husband and wife, in the antipasto tray cold cuts are always offered together with local **cheeses**. Here you can go crazy with the different kinds and ages. I recommend tasting two main versions: fresh, and therefore soft, or aged, and thus harder; as long as they are *pecorino senese* or *pecorino di Pienza* (sheep's cheese), and obviously Slow Food, which is a synonym of quality and attention to the whole line of traditional production. If you hear mention of *cacio marzolino* (from the Chianti or Crete areas), it's because this kind of *pecorino*, according to tradition, is produced in the month of March. Lastly, if you "dare," why not try a flavored cheese? You can choose among varieties such as truffle, pistachio, peppered, and *zafferano di San Gimignano DOP* (saffron from San Gimignano).

Ah, I almost forgot. Among appetizer trays you can always find the typical Tuscan *fettunta*: as the name implies (fetta = slice, unta = oily). It's a classic *bruschetta*, rubbed with garlic when it's oven toasted, then garnished with local Sienese extra virgin olive oil, salt and pepper. Now that we've mentioned oil, let's let two DOP (Protected Designation of Origin) brands inebriate us: *Chianti Classico DOP* and *Terre di Siena DOP*.

When it comes to **wines**, what should I say? It's embarrassingly hard to choose and would deserve its own chapter: the most notable come from vineyards in the hills surrounding Siena and nearby towns. The red *Brunello di Montalcino, Chianti, Nobile di Montepulciano* and *Chianti Classico are DOCG*, pairing well with red meat topped with truffle or mushrooms, or other flavorful first courses (meat sauces such as wild boar, hair and other wild game); the white *Vernaccia di San Gimignano* is more suitable to fish or first courses with a white sauce, such as the *zuppa di pane* or various cheeses.

And the famous *vin santo*, a scented and sweet dessert wine, with which Sienese love to end their evenings (if you love its smell, I recommend you visit the small town of *Montefollonico*, near *Torrita di Siena*). Among these wines you can pick with your eyes closed and as you please, without worrying about unpleasant surprises. As long as you don't drink too much...in that case its alcohol content could play some nasty tricks!

DINING WITH SIENESE FLAVORS
Quick Stops that Will Make your Mouth Water

Now that we've roused your appetite and you're already thinking about munching on some of the delights mentioned above, do you want to know what restaurants and pubs deserve a mandatory sampling?

For a quick and inexpensive lunch, **Il Grattacielo** (📞 +39 331 7422836) beneath the arch in Via dei Pontani is a simple place, with homemade Zero-kilometer dishes and a "down to earth" service (you'll understand first-hand what this metaphor refers to…). Among the various morsels offered for the day, ask if they have *acciughe* (truly exquisite anchovies). On the tables you can always find local cold cuts, hand-made marinated vegetables, *fagioli al fiasco* (beans inside a flask with oil, garlic, sage and other herbs and cooked over a grill or bagnomaria). If you like legumes, try out the *fagioli all'uccelletto*, beans flavored with garlic and sage, that in Tuscany were typical ingredients used when roasting small birds (*uccelletti*). If you want to enjoy them in a more robust dish, choose the *fagioli all'uccelletto con salsiccia fresca* (with fresh sausage served either whole or ground).

Osteria Il Vinaio (🔗 www.osteriailvinaio.it, 📞 +39 0577 49615) in Via Camollia offers tastes of all its typical products savored on paper napkins, following old tavern traditions. Its specials change daily: if you prefer rustic, traditional plates and you happen to come on the right day (usually Wednesdays), trust Bobbe and Davide, both brothers and owners, and order the *chiocciole di terra alla senese*, a plate of snails cooked in a wine and tomato sauce.

For a more informal, but "bio" lunch, check out **Oasi Verde** in Via di Pantaneto (🔗 www.oasiverdesiena.it, 📞 +39 0577 601697), a shop with both food and natural, vegetable and organic cosmetics where you can shop around or stay for lunch: from hot soups to rustic pizza with vegetables, from antique grain pastas to deli and bakery without using egg, butter, dairy or refined flours. The common thread is a cuisine privy of additives, straight from the field to the shelf. Massimo and

Simona will guide you to a personalized "formula", maybe surprising you with something good containing *miso* to taste with *beicha*, an excellent Chinese tea.

If you want to move up in price range, not far from here and near the cathedral, the **Taverna del Capitano** in Via del Capitano (☎ +39 0577 288094) sets a Palio atmosphere, with the photos hung on the walls (crooked on purpose) that describe Siena's tradition and its protagonists better than words. A few words with the owners will set you right at ease, among the flavors of their *ossobuco* and their traditionally made *ragù*. Many know this tavern as "i Tre Mori" (the three Mori), because running the place are father Franco, son Niccolò and daughter Carolina, a proud Sienese family, that between one plate and another delight you with ironic or salacious comments, for a meal from the "good old days" you will remember forever.

Staying near the Duomo, you can try **Ristorante San Desiderio** (☎ www.ristorantesandesiderio.com, ☎ +39 0577 286091). At first you might think you've got the wrong address, because the entrance seems that of an old Romanic church. Instead, after walking in, you'll find the best Tuscan cuisine, with its specialties of *pici* and *chianina* steak, then, mushrooms, wild boar, truffles; It's a romantic restaurant, ideal for a calm, slow meal. Appearances aren't misleading in this case, as this restaurant was once a medieval church. Ask Andrea, the owner, about its history.

Does today feel like a good day for trying something new? If so, let's reserve a table at **Salefino Vino e Cucina** (☎ www.salefino-siena.com/vino-e-cucina, ☎ +39 0577 287224), right in Piazza del Sale: a Parisian-style bistrot, with a delicate cuisine, that celebrates pairings of original flavors and plays on texture. You must try the *Uovo BT* (egg cooked at 67°C, so the exterior is solid while the yolk remains liquid), a true joy for your palate that balances just the right amount of liquid and crunch. Or, if it's on the menu, the *bottoni ripieni di quaglia* (small ravioli filled with quail ragù) and the *lingua di vitello tonné* (cow tongue covered in a creamy tuna and caper sauce). The team in the kitchen and the staff are young and full of talent, and trust me, I'm not the only one to recommend them: they can't pass unobserved now, not since

Gambero Rosso awarded them in their **Ristoranti d'Italia** guide under the category "best quality/price ratio."

For a genuinely Sienese meal, another must-taste place is the **Grotta di Santa Caterina** (www.ristorantebagoga.it, +39 0577 282208) in Via della Galluzza, better known as **"Bagoga's,"** name of the owner, Pierino Fagnani, ex-Palio jockey (in his hometown of Montalcino, *bagoga* comes from *albicocca*, or apricot). Menu highlights are the *tonno del Chianti* (Chianti tuna) e la *fagianella "alla Pia de' Tolomei"* (guinea-fowl), two house specialties. The first, the complete opposite of its name, is a tender filet of poached Cinta senese (local pig breed) served with chickpea cream. The latter is a delicious, slow-cooked guinea-fowl filled with veal and pork, black truffle, egg and grated cheese. Do you want a "whisker-licking" recommendation? Even if the *peposo "del Brunelleschi"* is a bestseller among the tourists, try the *gallo indiano*, a turkey thigh flavored with spices that remind us of *panforte*. I can still taste that delicate mix of coriander, juniper and cinnamon. To end your meal, *pecorino, miele e panpepato* (pecorino cheese, honey and panpepato) don't sound too bad, right? During the warmer months you can even enjoy your meal *al fresco*, at small tables on this typical hilly street.

Are you feeling creative this weekend? In Via di Pantaneto, long, colorful and ethnic street, **Osteria Babazuf** (www.osteriababazuf.com, +39 0577 222482) welcomes you. Although its name doesn't make any sense, its culinary sense does, believe me! Its motto is unique: *noi diamo il significante, voi date il significato* – "we give you a signifier, you give us its signified," as well as the picturesque frames on the walls, filled with food-themed images. Don't let the names of the plates scare you with their play on words, because Giovanni the chef and Marco the *maître* speak the same language: Italian ingredients (mushrooms, truffles, artichokes, etc.) plus excellence (only extra virgin olive oil) equals superb. Looking for appetizers? The menu offers seasonal options, but the *trine fatte in casa* (the artichoke carbonara sauce on this short-cut pasta is famous), the *polpo* (octupus) and *baccalà* (cod) made in several different ways are simple plates for refined palates.

My vegetarian friend always invites me to **L'Orto & un Quarto** (www.ortoeunquarto.it;   +39 0577 236223), the perfect solution for those who have given up on meat but not on taste! A ten-minute drive from the historical center, the location is truly captivating: look for the Strada di Montalbuccio, one of those country roads with a magnificent view on the city. A newly remodeled farmhouse surrounded by olive trees and complete with veranda will welcome you. Its vegetarian plates, employing seasonal vegetables from the garden in the back (making delicious *risotti*), are the most popular.

If you have a higher budget (€ 30/40), here are two restaurant recommendations that I would swear by. Near the Santuario di Santa Caterina, with a double entrance on both Via delle Terme and the suggestive Via dei Pittori, is the **Compagnia dei Vinattieri** (www.vinattieri.net,   +39 0577 236568). On the menu you can always find delicious handmade pasta (*ravioli* and *malfatti* beyond imagination) and *pici* for all seasons. Their two "battle horses": *bruschette di fagiano* (pheasant bruschetta) and *brasato* (braised meat). Under large brick arches and beautiful wooden beams, waiters flaunt the restaurant's slogan *"la vita è troppo breve per bere cattivo vino"* (life is too short to drink bad wine) and *modus operandi*, as the Vinattieri began as an *enoteca* (wine bar). Relaxed atmosphere, warm lights, hardwood floors: all the right ingredients for a high-quality lunch or dinner.

How, then, could you not be enchanted by the **Taverna di San Giuseppe** (www.tavernasangiuseppe.it,   +39 0577 42286)? Its entrance welcomes you under a frescoed vault, you breath in "Tuscan air": father and son, Marco and Matteo, know how to offer you the best of the Sienese tradition with some surprising quirks. Everything is exquisite, but if you want some advice, try the appetizer *tris della casa* (house trio): the *soufflé al pecorino fresco di Pienza e salsa di pere* (pecorino cheese soufflé with pear sauce) is hard to forget. You'll fall in love with their meat dishes: *ossobuco*, *cinghiale al latte* (wild boar), *lepre* (rabbit) o *tagliata all'olio buono* (sliced beef steak with olive oil). Looking for other specialties? The *funghi* (mushrooms) and *tartufi* (truffles) are on the menu year-round and are part of the reason the Taverna is so famous. If you prefer a lighter dish, the *stracci di pasta fresca alla zucca gialla estiva e zafferano* (homemade pasta strips with summer squash and saffron, grana cheese, thyme and marjoram) are extraordinarily delicate in their simplicity. End your meal with a pleasant surprise: *tiramisù con croccante di glucosio e nocciole sbriciolate* (*tiramisù* with crunchy caramel and hazelnut crumb topping). Imagine all this in an intimate space, with about 15 tables and an incredible *cantina*: it was an ancient Etruscan home carved by hand in the rock, later transformed into a Romanic church before becoming this family's well-stocked wine cellar.

Changing *genre*, if you're looking for the best fish in the city, you can start off by losing yourself in the romantic Vicolo delle Carrozze to discover **In Carrozza** (www.battisterosiena.com/in-carrozza-ristorante). A small, intimate restaurant with few tables (about 15 place settings), elegant brick and wooden architecture and large, ancient carriage wheels on the walls. The menu will delight you with a seven-course tasting of fish and other local products (50 euro fixed price menu, drinks excluded). Their specialty is the fried shrimp in a panko crust, accompanied with passion fruit mayonnaise. After dining here, you might imagine yourself going back in time by heading out into the night to exclaim "Ladies and gentlemen, to the carriage!"

Far from the more beaten paths, in Vicolo di Provenzano, inside a 17th century building we approach the **Enoteca Ristorante Tre Cristi** (www.trecristi.com, +39 0577 280608), recognizable by the sign which not only draws attention to the year 1830, but also reveals this place's history. Let Emanuele and Alessandro tell you about its name, because everyone in Siena know it as **Trattoria Tullio**. Then, most importantly, have them bring you the *crudo di mare* (appetizer with raw fish tartar, crustaceans and shellfish) and a first course of fish: these are the delicacies that made this place famous on the Michelin guide. If I were you, I would try the *menù degustazione*: three courses of "sea sampler" (€45) or the five courses of the "great sea menu" (65€). The main ingredients come mainly from the Tuscan coast, and the calm, silent atmosphere, with furniture from the 1920s and romantic candles on the tables, are widely renouned.

If, instead, you want to take a momento home from Siena, and stock up on edible souvenirs, then it's time to stop by the **Consorzio Agrario di Siena** (www.capsi.it), in front of Piazza Salimbeni: an impressive building that houses the best 0km products coming from a consortium of Sienese farmers. There we can do some food shopping or order a quick meal, with the pizzas and *ciaccini* (filled focaccias) from the **Menchetti** bakery and local cold cuts and cheeses. Right before leaving, don't pass up the fresh fruit sorbets from the **Gelateria BuonGusto of Pienza** (with unique, even vegan flavors), or maybe a delicious, fresh squeezed fruit juice, fruit smoothie, or fruit salad.

Sticking to our *gelato* theme, we reach the **La Vecchia Latteria** (+39 347 4746448) in the heart of Siena, just a few steps from the Duomo. You will not be disappointed by this artisanal *gelateria*: it's small, but quality and passion are guaranteed. Under the Fortezza Medicea, in the San Prospero neighborhood, the **Antica Cremeria Siena** (+39 333 5632501) proposes its specialty yogurt flavors.

For just the right coffee, I recommend a stop at the **Caffè Torrefazione Fiorella** (www.caffefiorella.it, +39 347 3532631), close to Piazza del Campo. It's just a few square meters, but more than enough for a quick sweet or salty breakfast accompanied by an excellent *caffè espresso*. You'll surely smell its aroma in Via di Città. The house mix is 80% Arabica and 20% Robusta, but you can also find Jamaican Blue Mountain and some South American Arabica. During the warmer months, try the summer "varieties": an iced *crema di caffè* or the coffee *granita* (with a dollop of whipped cream).

Nearby, in Via Banchi di Sopra, is the famous and much more spacious **Bar Nannini or Conca d'Oro** (www.nanninidolciecaffe.com, +39 0577 236009), a historic name that more than one hundred years ago introduced Siena to an innovative coffee machine that sent all the old percolators into storage. Together with our coffee, we have to let our sweet tooth take over and order a typical Sienese dessert: with *ricciarelli*, *cantucci*, *cavallucci* and *panpepato* you definitely won't be leaving with a dry palate. If, instead, you prefer a classic, the most loved specialties are the magnificent *meringhe* (meringues), hazelnut *bignès* and cream *brioches*.

Do you want to breathe in the smells of corks and tannins? Dive into the **Cantina in Piazza** in Via Stalloreggi 15 (www.cantinainpiazza. it, +39 0577 286595), a small wine bar where you can let Aimone Piazzi, the fantastic owner, advise you on choosing the best wines of the area. He can suggest the right "nectar" to bring home for dinner for any price range.

Another divine stop is the **Cantina del Brunello di Montalcino** (www.cantinadelbrunello.com, +39 0577 48446) in Via della Sapienza. A trip among great Tuscan wines (but not only) awaits you: the bottles can be tasted directly at this *enoteca*, thanks to the acclaimed guided tastings by Federico Pieri.

I've shown you some of the unbeatable places in this city, but culinary opportunities can also be found on the streets and in the many *piazze*. Between the end of October and early November, take advantage of two mouth-watering seasonal culinary appointments: the **Castagna in Carrozza** in the *Selva Contrada* (chestnut festival), filling the Vicolo delle Carrozze where you can munch on delicious *castagne* (chestnuts) or *frittelle di castagne* (fried chestnut flour), paired with wine, beer, chocolate, and mulled wine; or the **Novello nel Castello**, festival that takes place in the Castellare and streets of the *Civetta Contrada*, featuring the *vino novello* (new wine) and themed dinners that fill the central Piazza Tolomei.

During the rest of the year, instead, on Wednesday mornings take a nice stroll through the **mercato settimanale en plein air (weekly open-air market)** that takes place around the Fortezza Medicea. Right in the center of the city, just a few meters from the bus station: there, among the multicolored stands, not only can we browse typical clothing stands (the main attraction), but also some unexpected culinary gems directly from Southern Italy, especially if your taste buds are craving some *mozzarella di bufala* from Campania, Sicilian anchovies or delicious tomatoes from Puglia.

And so we've finished our tour of Sienese flavors. Being the great foodies that we are, this is just an appetizer. If you happen in Siena again, call me: for all the advice I've given, the least you could do is take me to dinner. Alright, I'll give you the honor of choosing the right place…so let your curious senses guide you to the aromas that creep through windows and doors, invading the streets! Let your wandering absorb the flavors as you go. As Latin will teach you, the verb *sapere*, today meaning "to know or have knowledge" originally meant "to have flavor." And if you've studied well, in our culinary travels together, it's time for you to experiment all your culinary knowledge. *Salute*, let's lift our glasses for a toast: "To Siena and all of its flavors…"

Chapter 7 / The Pilgrim

To Sacred from Profane

Following the footsteps of the great Sienese saints

I love noticing details on people. Eyes, hands, mouth. They reveal the character within each one of us. We can try to hide them, put up invisible armor to try to mask them, but at the end they are relentless, they come out and reveal who we really are. I've tried. When I was the head of my family's company, I tried to hide the lines that slowly kept growing on my forehead, but it was useless. The mirror noticed them first, cruel in its objectivity: one day it looked at me and shoved the truth in my face. That small detail didn't reveal who I was, rather who I was becoming. There was still time to change, and so I said, "Enough." I got rid of my business shoes and replaced them with a pilgrim's sandals, to finally bring back my true personality, and try to soften those lines on my face.

Eyes – Saint Bernardo Tolomei

Hundreds, thousands of eyes turned in one direction. Only those who had the honor of carrying it were denied that of admiring it. All the other eyes, however, could behold the beauty of the enormous altarpiece that shortly would be placed on the high altar of the Duomo of Siena. Among all those pupils straining to better observe the details of that *Maestà* that Duccio di Buoninsegna's paintbrush had the talent to design, there were also those of **Giovanni Tolomei**, probably already weak, that together with his companions had taken part in the solemn procession of June 9, 1311.

Shortly thereafter, that mild man would have decided to dedicate his life to the contemplation of God. For someone like me who believes in Providence and perceives the unknown in singular, everyday events, that solemn procession with the *Maestà* that dominated everything in its presence must have been a decisive moment in the life of who - in honor of Saint Bernard of Clairvaux - would have chosen to be renamed **Bernardo**. The choice of becoming a hermit was not his alone, but decided together with his lifelong friends Patrizio Patrizi and Ambrogio Piccolomini, two other last names synonymous with elite Sienese aristocracy.

Their joining Giovanni was a blessing for he who considered friendships his lifeblood. I can't imagine how their fathers reacted to the news: people used to traveling through Europe and coming in contact with the most noble families on the continent, able merchants, prisoners of the new banking system, they surely weren't pleased that three of their heirs were leaving to form a new hermit community. As if there weren't enough monks, both young and old, going around asking for charity during those times. But their fathers, forward-thinking in financial terms, and certainly a bit less in spiritual terms, didn't yet understand the difference that their sons were going to make, how they were destined to leave an indelible trace of their passing.

In the Spring of 1313, they distance themselves from the city and take up residence in one of the Tolomei family homes, where Giovanni, now called Bernardo, along with his companions, consolidate their possessions. Near this home, not many years later, one of the most important monasteries in Central Italy will be founded: Santa Maria di Monte Oliveto, later called **Monte Oliveto Maggiore**. It's here that I want to start my walk, in the shade of the cypress trees and the high walls of the abbey, to learn about the lives of these monks. None of them is young anymore; Bernardo, for example, is more than 40 years old. But their vocation is so sincere that right away others join their community of solitary seekers of God, that the Church then incorporated under the order of St. Benedict. In just a few years they become quite numerous: nobles and commoners, young and old, so much so to catch the attention of the bishop of Arezzo (whose territory included the monastery) who grants Bernardo and Patrizio the *Charta fundationis*, and thus March 26, 1319, the Benedictine Congregation of Monte Oliveto is officially born. The new monks choose to wear an entirely white frock, not only as a symbol of a pure soul, but also for other reasons. We are between the years 1318 and 1319. One day Bernardo, secluded in prayer, is presented with a vision: an enormous silver ladder appears in front of him, on the top of which he sees Jesus and the Virgin Mary in blinding white clothing; on the lower rungs are other monks dressed in white, climbing. There is a group of angels assisting them. Bernardo, almost awakening from his ecstatic state, runs to call his companions, and the news of the times confirm that others witnessed this prodigious apparition along with him. The white frocks of these monks are, from that moment on, characteristic of their order.

As I continue my walk that leads me to the abbey in Siena, I think about how Bernardo has given us an excellent example of humility. In the official act of founding the abbey, there is a precise request that the abbot is not to be elected for life, like the rest of Benedictine monasteries, but yearly. Everyone obviously wanted it to be Bernardo, but he turned down the role, not considering himself worthy, using the return of his eye disease as an excuse. Thus, his co-founder Patrizio Patrizi assumed the role. For Bernardo, humility also meant sacrifice; in 1321 his brothers' insistences convinced Bernardo that the humblest gesture would be to sacrifice himself for others and become their guide. So, at last he accepted, and was then re-elected abbot for the following 27 years.

The Black Plague took his life in 1348, along with 80 of his "white monks," all buried together in a common grave covered in limestone, as was used to avoid the spread of the disease. Had he stayed in his abbey, his life may have been saved. Instead, already older in age, he returned to Siena to stay in one of the order's monasteries near **Porta Tufi**, and there, caring for the sick, contracted the disease. As I reach the end of my contemplation of Bernardo, I encounter the walls of the city. The first part of my "pilgrimage" is finished, and I enter the city through **Porta Ovile**.

Hands - Saint Catherine of Siena

Can one be a giant without reaching 5'3"? Or rather, can one feel minuscule next to such a small woman? Yes, and her name is **Caterina da Siena**. When I chose to don pilgrim's clothing, my hands began to flip through lives of saints, searching for someone or something that could show me the way; Saint Catherine's accomplishments oriented my steps towards Siena. I am here because of her. I wanted to come here to discover who really was the woman that turned the tides of history with her work. I stop in front of the place where her **Santuario** is today, at the intersection of the steep **Costa di Sant'Antonio** and **Vicolo del Tiratoio**. In 1300 this was the home of dyer Jacopo Benincasa, and Lapa di Muccio dei Piagenti, whom God blessed with fertility. Caterina, in fact, was the 24th of 25 children. As a girl, although both witty and lively, she preferred to spend her time in prayer and watch her companions play their childish games from a distance. Caterina's destiny was entirely oriented towards God. As she grew up, she was persistent in wanting to join a religious order, but the total refusal of her family (who had set their sights on an ambitious wedding for her), forced her into a more "secular" solution with the nearby **Sorelle della Penitenza di San Domenico**, today the Third Order of Saint Dominic, an order of laic men and women. There was just one problem: these religious laypersons were also known as the "cloaked" for the long black cloak they wore over their white frocks, and since they weren't limited by any "vows" they lived in their homes, out in the world. Because of this, the order didn't admit women so young (still at an age when they could get married), and instead privileged honest widows or older women from rich families: Caterina was only sixteen!

Their rejection was categoric at first, but only because they didn't yet know the peaceful stubbornness of this girl, who never stopped requesting an interview. They finally accepted her request; two sisters of the order visited her, met her and heard her speak. Half an hour was enough to convince them. Thus, in a solemn "clothing" ceremony on a sunny Sunday of October, 1363, in the **Cappella delle Vòlte** (visitable from inside the **Basilica di San Domenico**), Caterina was accepted into the Order. Her mission could finally begin.

From that moment on, other than working together in the act of speaking to God, they began to assist the sick and needy. Word of her began to spread around the city: there were words of praise from those who saw the works of this young woman in positive light, but also bitter whisperings of those who couldn't accept that such a "simple" girl could possess such a high spirit. She prayed for everyone, acted for everyone: more and more Sienese began to follow her guidance.

There are so many of her works to mention. Walking along **Vicolo del Campaccio**, a brick tunnel that leads from the sanctuary to the basilica of San Domenico, I wonder how many times Caterina took this path, and stopped to contemplate the beauty of the view of the city from the top. I think about what I've read about her, in particular about what was reported in September 1370, when the very rich **Andrea di Naddino de' Bellanti** fell suddenly ill. Barely over 40 years old, he had earned a disputable reputation: troublemaker, swearer, blasphemer and womanizer. One time, after having lost a large sum of money gambling, he entered a church and started beating and eventually destroying a crucifix with his sword. Even with the decline of his health, he didn't slow down, refusing every contact with his confessor. Everyone in the city was talking about it: Andrea would have died without his last rites, a scandal unheard of for those times.

December arrived, and with it the day of Saint Lucy. The last hope for his wife and family was to turn to **Fra' Tommaso della Fonte**, Caterina's first confessor, who would have secretly asked for Caterina's help. As soon as the request reached her, she immediately withdrew herself in prayer. This was Caterina's strength: go directly to the Source, in such a way that the lost soul's mind would be changed not by words, that would have fallen on deaf ears, but directly by the Lord, who surely would have known what to do. That same night Andrea had a vision in his sleep, and upon awakening his face had completely changed. He calmly asked for a priest to confess him. In town they were calling it a miracle. Caterina had never once spoken to him yet was rewarded with saving his soul.

The Bellanti family were not the only ones to experience a miraculous conversion. Even the Tolomei, the same family of Saint Bernardo, witnessed the effects and strength of Saint Catherine's hands, offering both grace and mercy. It was **Madonna Rabe Tolomei**, well-known figure in the family, a rigid and strict woman, who went knocking on Caterina's door in Fontebranda. She kneeled in front of the "commoner" and, in front of her compassionate gaze, opened her tormented heart. Her sons, who should have been upholding the good name of the family, were instead agonizing her. Her daughters, Ghinoccia and Francesca, were superficiality impersonated. They spent exorbitant sums of money on dresses, cosmetics and perfume, flaunting their vanity. Then there was Giacomo, the oldest. As a young man, he had killed two men with his bare hands during one of the many fights he had been involved in. He boasted about his recklessness and was disdainful to those who cautioned him. Caterina listened to Madonna Rabe for hours, then agreed to meet the daughters. The appointment was set for the same day, in the **Chiesa di San Cristoforo**, directly in front of the Tolomei family home. We can't know what Caterina said to the young ladies, but when they left the church that day, they had put spoiled behavior behind them and eventually requested to join the Third Order of Saint Dominic.

During this short period of time, Giacomo, the firstborn, was away from Siena. As soon as he heard what had happened and how his sisters had been convinced to wear the habit, he no sooner came back to the city. While he rode his horse, he planned his revenge by putting all his anger towards she who had dared interfere in his family's business, calling Caterina "Fontebranda's bigot." When he reached Siena, it was the middle of the night and Madonna Rabe was there waiting for him. In the meantime, she had sent another message to Caterina, who then spoke with Fra' Tommaso, asking him to bring a message to Giacomo. Then, as always, she withdrew in prayer. As the friar knocked on the door his knees were shaking. He didn't know how this young rebel would have reacted at seeing his frock. Giacomo, in fact, was seething in rage and refused any sort of reform. Suddenly, as if under a spell, his expression changed, so much so that even the friar no longer recognized him. If his eyes were incredulous at what they were seeing happen to Giacomo, that which his ears heard afterwards made him almost lose his senses. This young Tolomei was slapping himself, calling himself stupid and accusing himself of all his sins. At the same time, he began to praise God and congratulate his sisters on having dedicated their lives to the Lord. Madonna Rabe was filled with joy. Caterina, at the same time, rejoiced alone in her room. From that day on, Giacomo became a mild-mannered man, a diligent husband and towards the end of his life even asked to wear the frock of the Third Order of Saint Dominic.

There are so many other sources that narrate acts of conversion or miraculous events tied to Caterina. With time, her persuasive talents became so famous that a group of people, known as the **Bella Brigata (Beautiful Brigade)**, accompanied her everywhere and wrote down what she said. Her trip to Avignon is also historically famous, during which, after having beseeched Pope Gregory XI in letters, she herself was at his side when he finally ended the so-called "papal captivity." So many gestures, so many actions, until that final Sunday in April 1380, when her soul reunited forever with her celestial groom.

I stand up from the bench where I had been admiring Siena from **Camporegio** and begin to climb the stairs of the majestic **Basilica di San Domenico** (www.basilicacateriniana.it). Inside, past the previously mentioned Cappella delle Vòlte, **Saint Catherine's head and right thumb** are preserved and displayed. She who with her hands changed the course of history.

Mouth - Saint Bernardino of Siena

This city seems imbued with spirituality. Every corner, every glimpse of a landscape, in fact, provokes reflection. I've reached another of Siena's basilicas, **San Francesco**. In a strange coincidence, this church was founded together with the birth of Giacomo Tolomei in 1272 and strengthened with Saint Catherine in 1347. The year 1380 is also the year another great Sienese saint was born, who opened his eyes for the first time in Massa Marittima, where his father, **Tollo degli Albizzeschi**, was governor. The name pronounced on the day of his baptism in the cathedral was Bernardino, and that child was destined to become one of the most fervent and talented speakers in all medieval Christian history. Bernardino, orphaned at six years of age, was sent up to Siena and entrusted to his aunts, owing to them the opportunity to study, gain knowledge and become known for his lively way with words. At 22 he donned the Franciscan habit and, thanks to his eloquence, in a short time became famous for his sermons. Many of those who heard him speak noted a particular detail about his face: his mouth was like a line on his face, almost lipless. The bald and slightly pointed head didn't do much to distract from this feature: from that mouth came fervent words that raptured, if not excited, any spectator.

From Piazza San Francesco, after visiting the Oratory dedicated to him in 1450, the year of his canonization, and then frescoed by painters like Sodoma, Girolamo del Pacchia or Beccafumi (today also housing the **Diocese Museum of Sacred Art**), I head towards Piazza del Campo. I have a particular painting on my mind as I walk, one that is almost a photograph, as I saw it the other day at the **Museo dell'Opera del Duomo**. The painter, Sano di Pietro, portrays Saint Bernardino standing high on a wooden pulpit and preaching in front of the Palazzo Pubblico in front of a large crowd that seems to be hanging on his every word. Next to him are stands, where the city's most prominent figures are seated. The people in front, men to the left, women to the right, and separated by a red cord, to limit certain "distractions" during the sermon, or, as Bernardino said, so that one's or the other's eyes can't probe any more than they should.

I stop and try to listen. It's as if I'm there, right in front, as if I can see those lips move. His voice is clear in my ears; I sit and…

Declina a malo, et fac bonum: inquire pacem (*Psalmus XXXIII*).

Turn from evil and do good, seek peace (Psalm XXXIII).

My beloved citizens, these are the words of the prophet David: Turn from evil and do good, seek peace. Everything that our city and its people need is written here, and I will say it to you: Oh, people of Siena, leave evil and do good.

Until just a few hours ago I was more dead than alive, I suffered incredible fever pains and I could barely stand. Now, in front of you, I feel so strong I could withstand a duel. I don't know how this happened, but the words of this Psalm truly reassured me. And this message must be clear and reach everyone: seek harmony.

Don't deceive yourselves into thinking that my words are meant for your friends or your enemies; they are for everyone: women, men, rich, poor. Everything begins here (he opens his mouth, sticks out his tongue and indicates it with his finger): from slander.

Let's divide the prophet's sentence into three parts. First: **Turn from evil.** *Second:* **do good.** *Third:* **seek peace.**

Let's begin from the first, about which I want to give you three warnings. We must first wake up, be vigil; then we must decide to flee from bad actions; lastly, we must practice doing good.

It's never too late to repent our own sins, but it is never too soon to use our conscience. If you feel in debt, to God and to your brothers, and you want to fix your evildoings, do it! If someone realizes they've taken the wrong road, that is the moment to stop, turn around, follow the right path. And make sure your actions are full, not empty. Full are the actions that illuminate from the grace of God, done freely and solely out of love for one's neighbor. Empty are, instead, the actions that may seem inspired by virtue, but are surrounded by hypocrisy and vainglory. Those who act in this way do exactly as those who fill their own sack with smoke. This is what is meant by the first point, as I said: **Turn from evil.**

Second part of the plea: **do good;** *even in this case I will divide this point in three parts. First, listen to good. Second, keep in mind the good you hear. Third, and most importantly, do good.*

Listen? We can do it in two ways: first with our ears, then with the intent to remember. Listen to this example: there was a holy father near here who lived separated from the world in a small house in the woods. A young helper lived with him, who had the flaw of not remembering anything. One day the old man took him aside and told him, "Do you see that pan over there that you use to cook fish? Go get it for me." Then he took some water and boiled it. When it was hot enough, he asked the young man to pour the boiling water on the dirty and greasy pan. "Look now," he said, "tell me if it's cleaner than before." Seeing the young man nod, he asked him to repeat the action over and over until the pan was completely clean. Then he turned to him and began, "You say you don't remember anything? Because your mind is dirty and greasy, just like the pan was. Go and wash it with the only water that purifies the heart, the word of God, and you'll see what effect it has." Here, then, is the remedy, my people. If you will let that water run over you, then doing good will be natural, spontaneous, effortless.

The third part says: **seek peace**. *Seek peace, city of Siena, seek peace. To do this, we need to flee from three capital flaws: being cold, being hard, being blind.*

Cold people do not find pleasure in the things created; they remain impassive in front of the beauty of the Lord's works. They do not enjoy life, and thus do not look for harmony, which is the first step towards peace. Hard people don't believe they are neither seen nor heard, they don't understand that their actions are under the eyes of God. Stealing, killing, violence, slander, gossip, fighting, jealousy. The last, the blind, are those who do not see the benefits of peace, which leads to carrying out the will of the Lord and benefits the entire human race.

So, open your eyes!

And so, I truly open them. I am still here, in Piazza del Campo, and it's already evening: I didn't notice how much time had passed. Saint Bernardino's words are resounding in my head. Even though they were directed at those who lived in the city in 1427, they seem to be relevant to everyone even today. Most importantly, they seem relevant to me.

TOUR OF THE SEVEN CHURCHES

Have you ever wondered where the proverb *"giro delle sette chiese"* (tour of the seven churches) comes from? We will have to go all the way back to 1600 and Saint Philip Neri. The famous giro, tour, was an itinerary of several kilometers that went to the most important churches in Rome, so demanding that it took pilgrims at least two days to complete it. Even in Siena you can complete a rich tour among churches and monasteries, naturally covering less distance. Here are the stops you can't miss.

Let's start with the **Collegiata di Santa Maria in Provenzano**, that takes its name from the district where the Sienese war captain Provenzano Salvani resided. Here a terracotta half bust of the Virgin Mary is housed, that, since its construction in 1611 has been above the high altar, while before was placed along the street of this neighborhood. Legend has it that one day a Spanish soldier got the idea to shoot the sculpture, but the shoulder rifle exploded in his hands, converting him (in the "official" version), or killing him (in the popular version). From that moment on, other than subject of veneration, the image became a clear symbol of resistance. For Siena it is without a doubt the second most important place of worship in the city, so much so that in honor of this image of Mary the tradition of the Palio on July 2 was born.

Taking the steep street that leads to Piazza Tolomei, we arrive in front of the small but important church of **San Cristoforo**, dating late 11th century. In the Middle Ages, before the Palazzo Pubblico was built, inside this church the Republic of Siena's General Council would meet, the most important assembly for Sienese citizens. It was right here that the expedition against the Florentines in 1260 was decided, that would have led to the well-known Battle of Montaperti. The adjacent courtyard is characteristic of the 12th century, accessible from Via del Moro. Here you can find another small gem, a tombstone that marks the burial of the great medieval poet Cecco Angiolieri right under these bricks.

Not far, in Via del Porrione, is the church of **San Martino**, place of worship dating back to the 7th century, expanded and remodeled various times before its current baroque appearance. The inside is a

Latin cross, with one nave and a cupola decorated with frescoes by Annibale Mazzuoli. But the real treat is a solemn *Nativity* by Domenico Beccafumi, active during the first half of the 16th century and last (along with Sodoma) of the great Sienese school of art that, in three centuries, embellished numerous churches and buildings with masterpieces. There is another painting that some look past, but after a closer look reveals an authentic masterpiece. Even though it has been darkened by fire, the unmistakable brushstrokes of Guercino come out in his *Martyrdom of Saint Bartholomew*.

A detour in our route brings us to one of the oldest parts of the city, in the Castelvecchio district. Passing by, if it wasn't for the doorbell we would almost miss it, with its hidden entrance on the street, even though the **Convent of San Niccolò al Carmine** represents one of the most interesting religious places in Siena. Erected by the Caramelites in the 13th century, the convent incorporated the previous church of San Niccolò, one of the first built in the city. Many notable works of art are preserved inside here, among which one of Beccafumi's masterpieces, the *Fall of the Rebel Angels*. Continuing past the Cappella del Santissimo Sacramento (Chapel of the Holy Sacrament), the church preserves a treasure of antique devotion: the *Madonna of the Cloaks*, a byzantine style table dating to the first half to the 13th century, on which children used to hang small ornamental cloaks as thanks for graces received from the Virgin Mary.

Heading south we search out the **Basilica dei Servi**; we can see it start to come into view through the narrow streets of the opposite hill. It was erected on a small hill where monks from the new Order of Servants of Mary (Servite Order) established themselves mid-12th century, constructing, with the help of the city of Siena and the rich Tolomei family, the convent and new place of worship where the antique Church of San Clemente (the official name: San Clemente in Santa Maria dei Servi) once stood. The inside quickly became one of the most important places in the city dedicated to Mary, you can find the *Madonna del Bordone* by Coppo di Marcovaldo (the Florentine artist painted this piece in exchange for his freedom after being taken prisoner during the Battle of Montaperti), *The Incarnation of the Virgin* by Bernardino Fingai and the *Madonna of Mercy* by Matteo di Giovanni. Its majestic pipe organ, Mascioni opus 370, although recently constructed in 1925, deserves mentioning.

We turn back towards the center of the city, heading towards the impressive **Basilica di San Francesco**, gigantic, almost disproportionate, compared to the buildings surrounding it. Construction began in the 13th century and expanded over the next two centuries. It represents an ideal synthesis between the original Romanic style and the later gothic style. Inside its walls a "permanent miracle" is housed. Its story brings us back in time to the night of August 14, 1730, when a thief entered the church and stole a precious Eucharist box full of blessed hosts that he disposed of right away. Found three days later in the Collegiata di Provenzano, a solemn procession brought the hosts back to San Francesco. The miracle? From that day on, instead of deteriorating like any typical unleavened bread, they are still there, intact. From that day on, 293 calendars have come and gone and those wafers, analyzed more than once, even recently by a team of experts, have yet to change.

The other large basilica, reference point for pilgrims of Saint Catherine from all over the world, is **San Domenico**, rising on top of the Camporegio hill. Built between the 13th and 14th centuries, it maintains its strict and massive architectural style of the mendicant orders, that used humble materials for their churches, and offers an amazing view of the Duomo, Torre del Mangia and the opposite hill. At night it seems suspended in air. The church contains relics of Saint Catherine (head and right thumb), conserved in a Renaissance chapel that was frescoed by Sodoma and other great artists.

The seven churches are now behind us, but our tour mustn't exclude the **Synagogue**, temple that boasts an important tradition and represents one of the rarest examples of rococo and neoclassicism in Siena. The existing building, in **Vicolo delle Scotte**, was inaugurated in 1786 and then restored in 1902. The inside is magnificently decorated and houses a museum of texts and images that commemorate the most significant moments of Siena's Jewish community, present here since 1229.

Chapter 8 / The Explorer

Hidden Treasures

Seeking out unexpected worlds

Whenever there was a costume party, I always chose to dress as Indiana Jones; I liked walking in the world-famous archeologist's shoes. As time went on, I started to understand that visiting a place didn't require boots and a helmet to make me feel like a first-rate explorer, forced to find my way into narrow holes in search of unexplored treasures. Having the right "eye," instinct and desire for the thrill of a new discovery was enough.

Map in hand, all you need to do is lift your head to realize that in Siena appearances can deceive, so you need to look closer. What seems like a regular balcony, for example, turns out to be a *sporto*, or protrusion. I'm in **Vicolo di Coda**, heading towards **Via del Rialto** when I notice one: no one knows what its true purpose was. For some, a *sporto* was used as a connection between two buildings, so that nobles weren't forced to go down the stairs, towards the commoners; others believe that it was a system of defense, so that arrows or boiling oil could be hurled onto enemies; my favorite is the third hypothesis, that from a central hole, at night all the "biological material" from the day was "unloaded." A sort of medieval toilet.

When I turn towards **Vicolo dell'Oro**, on my right, I notice another peculiarity on the facades of the buildings, like arched ledges, recognizable signs of an architectural style that characterizes the **Salicotto** district. Its curious name derives from the words salato (salted) and cotto (cooked), because in this area they produced cured meats and preserved salt in enormous warehouses, almost as valuable as a bank's vault (today called the **Magazzini del Sale**, popular space for art shows and events).

Salicotto is also the historical ghetto district. I set out in **Vicolo delle Scotte**, a narrow alley that reminds me of a secret tunnel, decorated with arches and flowered balconies. The name *Scotte* refers to the Jewish holiday "Sukkot" and in fact, at number 14 on this street is the entrance to the Synagogue. Combing this area, I discover other interesting street names, such as **Vicolo della Fortuna** (Fortune street), next to Vicolo della Manna (Manna, or Godsend Street).

Walking down **Via degli Archi** I lose myself among the narrow street openings through which I can admire the Torre del Mangia over the rooftops. The steep Vicolo di Coda opens up to **Via di Salicotto**, a long street that connects Piazza del Campo with the southern part of the city. I stop briefly in **Piazza del Mercato**, that looks over the **Valle di Porta Giustizia (Valley of Justice Gate)**, famous in the Middle Ages because here is where capital punishment was carried out. Prisoners in chains exited the prison under the Palazzo Pubblico and reached the valley passing through Via dei Malcontenti (Street of the Displeased), its name explaining well enough the state of mind of those condemned to death.

This place also offers us a special view of a large portion of Siena's **walls**. Various circles of the walls were built, and later widened as the city grew; I like to look at them and try to understand their layout, even beyond what I can see. I love touching them, almost caressing them, as if it were the trunk of a century-old oak. As a boy I often played at my grandmother's feet while she sat in her armchair, feeling consoled by her silent protection. Siena's walls are just like a grandmother: wise, solid and protective.

Because of their privileged stature, they are the owners of the city gazing lovingly upon the city like those who are watching their grandchildren grow up: kilometers of stone that reveal the history of Siena more than any other street, erected by their people to render it an unconquerable fortress, and that, despite periods of unjustified neglect, have survived the centuries almost entirely intact.

While I try to follow them and discover some proof of the various eras of construction, I notice some young people that, shovel in hand, are cleaning up a portion. I get closer, but I soon realize something strange: they don't have the typical Sienese accent. Indeed, they are speaking in English with a notable American accent. This is how I meet **SIS Intercultural Study Abroad's** students, American students that have been contributing to the **Associazione Le Mura's** efforts for years. Together with many good-willed Sienese, they dedicate their time to taking care of those antique stones and bricks, containing a thousand shades and colors, filled with that brilliant green from the tufts of grass growing in its cracks: I recognize wild caper plants, ivy, and the well-known **verbena**, protagonist of Sienese folk songs and imagery.

L'ORTO DE' PECCI
a green oasis in the middle of the city

There is a place in Siena where the city and countryside unite and embrace: this is the **Orto de' Pecci** (www.ortodepecci.it). Following the principle that there are always more stories to hear and there is always something to discover, I let **Maura** take my hand and guide me to discover one of the wonders of the city, at only 300 meters from Piazza del Campo. Orto de' Pecci is an uncontaminated oasis where you can relax, comforted by the green of the medieval garden, face to face with animals, right under Piazza del Mercato. Maura is one of the organizers of the daily maintenance, managed by the social organization **La Proposta**, an Italian non-profit organization that assists people with social and professional (re)integration. The Orto has two souls: the *park*, open to everyone and particularly recommended for anyone looking for a relaxing walk or a quiet place to read outdoors, and the **ristorante con pizzeria**, where you can eat "zero meter" vegetables grown in the surrounding garden.

What makes this place extraordinary are the *gente dell'orto*, people of the garden, as they call themselves. Made up of approximately 30 staff and 15 collaborators in social reintegration that, like a big team, dedicate their time to taking care of the garden and the organization's other initiatives: from its restaurant to its many cultural activities for young and old alike, from caring for the animals to the cultivation respecting the garden's medieval techniques.

Here I am with Maura, in front of a glass of ruby-red wine, as she tells me about her unique colleagues: Fabione, who opens the Orto's gates every morning and then goes around in his truck collecting the city center's recycling. Or about Bruno, who feeds the goats and, immersed in nature, dedicates his time to his greatest passion, his animals. She also tells me about someone who unfortunately has passed, Roberto Caracciolo, known as Robertone, one of the first collaborators. A lover or verses, he used to recite stanzas he composed that described the soul of this place:

«all'Orto de' Pecci siamo rotolati, siamo disagiati e handicappati, tra corvi, conigli e merli, siamo comandati dai friscelli. Con Tursi e Caracciolo e Bielli, lavoriamo noi persone. E questa è la canzone di Robertone».

"At the Orto dei Pecci, we are spun, we are awkward and handicapped, among crows, rabbits and blackbirds, we are ordered around by flour dust. With Tursi and Caracciolo and Bielli, we work. And this is the song of Robertone."

You can see, it's not just the Orto that's unique with its view and its restaurant, but those who work there...

If the protagonist of **Alice in Wonderland** were to wake up in a real city, she certainly would choose this place as a natural setting for her adventures. She could speak with the rabbits, take a selfie with a peacock, sing along with the birds, play ball in the grass, whisper poetry to the fruit trees. Then maybe she would take flight on one of the many hot air balloons that land in the Orto several times a year, making dreams come true for both young and old (www.tuscanyballooning.it).

I head towards **Via Sant'Agata.** I want to admire that valley from above and appreciate its contours. I already have the perfect place in mind: at the **Orti dei Tolomei (Tolomei Gardens),** from which one can enjoy some of the most suggestive views of the city and whose trails encourage a stop for reflection. Finally I can put my spare notes from my notebook in order.

On the other side of the park, I am looking forward to visiting another one of the treasures that pushed me to visit Siena. A place of culture, research, discovery: the prestigious **Accademia dei Fisiocritici** (www.fisiocritici.it), its entrance right in front of the Sant'Agostino lawn, in **piazzetta Silvio Gigli**, in what was once a Camaldolese convent from the 12th century. This institution was founded at the end of the 17th century by Pirro Maria Gabbrielli, doctor and instructor at the Ateneo Senese, who felt the need to create a space to "scrutinize and investigate with judgement the secrets of nature and, almost like judges, discard that which for the natural sciences is false in order to better understand that which is true;" as stated in the Constitution of the Accademia from the end of the 17th century. These were truly explorers of "truth" through science, inspired by that revolutionary experimental method made of trials and verifications conducted in a laboratory that guided the greatest minds of the time, starting with Galileo Galilei.

Fisiocritici were scholars, and their group included names such as Sallustio Bandini, Giovanni Battista Morgagni, Carlo Linneo, Francesco Algarotti, Leonardo Ximenes, Lazzaro Spallanzani, Alessandro Volta, Paolo Mascagni, George Cuvier, Joseph-Louis Lagrange, Bettino Ricasoli, Louis Pasteur and Robert Koch. In the 18th century, the Accademia become a point of reference for hygiene and healthcare with pioneered studies on vaccines, and, later, for many other disciplines. The name *Fisiocritici* began to circulate in the cultural clubs around Europe, becoming a synonym of prestige, thanks to its commitment to scientific research and diffusion of knowledge. Their mission is still alive today, as they continue to nominate new *Fisiocritici* every year, carry out didactic activities with local schools, organize events, shows and congresses, even in collaboration with the University of Siena and many other cultural institutions. Within the Accademia you can peruse a scientific library, an archive with thousands of documents that attest the numerous results in the scientific field obtained within these walls, and visit the **Museum of Natural History**. That's where I'm headed.

As soon as I enter, my attention is immediately drawn to the display case that contains a rare piece: a perfectly preserved fossilized mammoth tusk. Just enough time to catch my breath that my eyes have already caught sight of the inner courtyard, where, on the other side of the glass, a gigantic **fin whale skeleton** (found on a beach near Piombino in 1974, since then becoming the symbol of this museum) is displayed in all its splendor. I could stay there for hours just admiring it; I get a bit closer but other pieces of treasure distract me and I can't help but investigate.

The expositive structure of this place perfectly replicates the nature of museums in the 19th century, where everything was amassed and presented to the visitor with the intent of stupefying them; nothing at all in comparison to modern museums that isolate the most important works in separate rooms dedicated to them. Here enormous display cases show off discoveries and collections together, in a sequence of *mirabilia*, that for me represent an infinite source of findings: on the ground floor alone we come across fossils (yes, Siena was once covered by the sea, as the whale vertebra found in Vicolo di Tone can attest), minerals and rocks of every kind, including the famous *Terra di Siena*. On the same floor you can visit the uniquely interesting room filled to the brim with terra-cotta mushrooms, dating to mid-19th century, painted with extreme precision and used for didactic purposes, so as to assure a safe and conscientious gathering and use by the city's population.

Moving around the rooms in complete awe, I notice the entrance to the auditorium, where another rarity is kept: a rather particular **meridian**, called a **Fisiocritic Heliometer**, initially in the previous location of the Accademia in Via della Sapienza (the original location was inside the Santa Maria della Scala) and then reconstructed in the current location. Why particular? First, because it's "a dark room" built indoors, though more importantly, when it was built in the beginning of the 18th century it was one of only four existing of its kind in Europe. Another interesting piece, in the adjacent room, a **comparison stone** is displayed, a hard rock against which objects of gold and silver were rubbed to test their authenticity. While searching for a symbol to represent the *Fisiocritici* as seekers of truth, they decided to portray this in their crest, a symbol still used today to identify this institution.

I'm confronted with a choice: go below ground or up to the next floor. If I choose the former, moving through the tunnels dug in the sandstone, I will have the opportunity to admire a small collection of telescopes and Armillary spheres, before reaching the circular cistern that once collected rain water and today houses an original electronic **planetarium**. I could also visit the area dedicated to the study of **botanics**, where I could examine collections of seeds, resins, woods and an herbarium dating to the second half of the 18th century. Attributed to Biagio Bartalini, it represents the perfect merging of painting and scientific study: excellent for the delicacy of the lines and colors, the 30 paintings are realized in watercolor on watermark paper.

Nonetheless, my legs have already begun the ascent to the first floor, where, in a beautiful gallery, an endless number of **stuffed examples** of animals are waiting for me: thousands of birds, hundreds of mammals, reptiles, fish, insects, mollusks, various marine invertebrates and even a collection of parasites conserved in alcohol. A display that, for me, has the inebriating power of a lavish dinner.

A ramp of stairs leads to another room, where I find something truly unique: this is the section of the museum dedicated to the great

Tuscan scientist **Paolo Mascagni**, pioneer in the description of the lymphatic system and of anatomic representation through illustrations that, calling them peculiar is without a doubt a euphemism. Finding yourself directly in front of an immense **map of the human body**, created for facilitating the work of medicine students, complete with 44 life-sized boards, is exciting to say the least.

And that's not all. Next to this *Anatomia universa* (1823-1831), there is a collection of vases injected with mercury containing human anatomical pieces, you can admire the results of Mascagni's tireless studies of the lymphatic system. After having explored this museum, I can finally understand the reason why it has been listed in the circuit of *Google Arts and Culture* that gives users all over the world the possibility to virtually access a cultural itinerary that spans geology and botanics, zoology and anatomy.

I leave the museum and, as I stand in Piazzetta Silvio Gigli, I notice the musical arrangement engraved in the stones. What is it? One of the installations of contemporary art entitled "**Tempo Zulu**," stones that in 2004 were added to the streets all around the city. Time will eventually erase its traces, so make sure to look for them while they are still visible! There are ten others in the historical center. This one is called *Arborescences* and is fruit of the meeting of two artists that imagined a hypothetical musician that, passing by here, made this arrangement come alive.

The name of the work is a homage to the **Orto Botanico** (☏ +39 0577 235407), just a few steps away, at number 4 in **Via Mattioli**, a place in which the sounds of nature penetrate the city. I can't not cease the moment: a heavy iron gate welcomes me, the writing "Regio Orto Botanico" still legible, an evident sign of the move to this place during the Resurgence, even though its historical roots are much deeper. The stairs lead to an enchanted garden, where the most varied species of plants and trees live together. Its area, spanning from Porta Tufi to Porta San Marco, all within the perimeter of the medieval walls, occupies two and a half hectares in the slope of the **Valley of Sant'Agostino**. Its location is particularly fortunate as it faces south-west, and the above hill is a natural protection from northern winds. Time stops, at least for me it does. I go from one arrangement to the next, trying to remember the names of the plants that I recognize and helping myself, when I can't, to the detailed labels that dictate common name, scientific name and family classification. The two artificial terraces on the sides of the main building are overflowing with medicinal and edible plants; their inebriating aroma accompanies me as I start down one of the trails in the park, divided by various flowerbeds on more than one level.

Looking around you, this place gives the impression of living in a microcosm in which all the existing species live together: with a quick turn of the head, I move from tropical to mountain species, without counting the vast selection of bushes typical of the Tuscan ecosystem. Grapevines, olives and fruit trees are the background of this **Podere (old farmhouse)**, another zone that extends to the walls. Before going down, though, I must stop at the greenhouses: the **lemon tree house** filled with flowers and citrus trees; the **antique greenhouse** that reproduces the hot, humid climate of the rainforest; the **tepidarium**, which displays tropical species and recreates desert and semidesert-like atmospheres of certain areas in America and Africa. Next to me I notice a man with glasses who is slowly and calmly moving among the flowerbeds; I ask around and find out that there is even a tactile itinerary made specifically for the accompanied seeing-impaired; we sit on a bench in the sun and I enjoy the tales told by my new companion.

ON THE HUNT FOR MYSTERIES

Every city has its "fears:" legends whispered in your ears passed down through time, speaking of ghosts, witches and vampires. In my backpack, my *Magical Guide to Siena* is always within reach. Like a "spiritual guide," author Massimo Biliorsi takes us on four different tours: the first, smelling of sulfur and sounding of the jingling of old coins, leads us from the **Basilica of San Domenico to the Magnifico residence**. The second, among wolves and cursed fountains, from Piazza Provenzano leads to the valley of **Porta Giustizia**. A third explores the path from **Piazza del Campo to Via della Diana**: you don't need to take any precautions, just watch out for ghosts. The last twists and turns outside of the historical center get you lost in the fountains of Ovile, touches the Basilica dell'Osservanza and ends at the ossuary of Montaperti.

The werewolves of the *Fonte del Casato* and *Fonte della Sapienza*, the ghost river Diana, or the spirits that move around the cursed Follonica fountain: if water is one of the common threads of these strange legends, many others are magical figures that you may run into on the streets of the city. You can hear werewolves howling in Vicolo degli Orefici, glance witches lurking around Via del Porrione and Via del Rialto, hear noises and footsteps of Brother Giorno's ghost at the Botanical Gardens, meet the healer of the Magnifico Palace and speak face to face with the Orto de' Pecci's vampire, in the enchanted valley of Porta Giustizia.

These folklore tours are not for the faint at heart, but recommended for the adventurous soul who, in a night of thunder and lightning, gets off the couch with flashlight and magnifying glass in hand.

I must have been dreaming. I can hear water around me, flowing around the Orto in various ways: small tubs, mini lakes, ponds and streams. Water has been a sweet obsession for Sienese since the Middle Ages. The Government of the Nine had even been so forward thinking to understand that only a capillary water system would have brought the city prosperity. Already in 1226 the term "buctinus" was being used, referring to the barrel vaults (series of side by side arches) typical of these underground tunnels: a network of 25 kilometers of aqueducts that still supply water to Siena's historical fountains.

I decide to take on this new adventure and come to the entrance of the **Bottino maestro di Fonte Gaia,** built around the year 1300. The underground descent is quick and the humidity invades me. The sound I hear is that of the *gorello*, a small channel where rainwater and other underwater veins meet.

I start walking down the first part and notice that the height and width are regular and consistent (height three arm lengths and width one and a half: these were the instructions for the master builders); I remember having read that the creative medieval architects used an instrument called **archipendulum,** useful for maintaining the same degree of slope for water flow. Water, in fact, was not supposed to flow too quickly, otherwise they wouldn't have been able to collect it correctly; neither was it supposed to flow too slowly, because sediments would have accumulated and blocked the channel's flow. I wonder what it took to create them using the technology of the times: the **guerchi,** the name given to those who labored during the realization of the *bottini,* sometimes gave their lives to this intricate series of tunnels, an unbearable job not only because of the scarce visibility and low temperatures, but also for the exhausting nature of the work. These specialized workers were forced to dig all day long in semi-darkness, ended up not being able to stand daylight, and thus their name is derived from ciechi, blind.

Continuing along the tunnel I notice some small openings above, **smiragli,** used for letting light and air in. Certainly useful, but they had to be extremely cautious in creating them, because one wrong move could have caused a deadly collapse. In addition to creating channels with the correct slope, purification basins (**galazze**) were also part of the plan, where water arrived and had time to naturally purify before continuing down the channels.

I continue my exploration of this engineering "miracle," that had become the lymphatic system of the city.

At a certain point I realize I've lost track of the main tunnel; I'm not one who panics easily, but I have to admit that all these dark tunnels are not helping. The silence surrounding me sends a shiver down my spine; the only sound the light trickling of the water and what sounds like….yes, those are footsteps behind me. I turn around and a small, toothless, likable elf appears in front of me. He accuses me of having disturbed his slumber and introduces himself as **Fuggisole** (**Sunescape**), the spirit of the *bottini*, who often reoccurred in the tales of the guerchi, and who, according to the workers, had the evil power of poisoning anyone who encountered him with his deadly breath. I keep my distance as he tells me to not believe any of the legends about him, that he's never hurt anyone. Rather, like with me, he helps people to find the right way towards the exit. Before disappearing into the shadows, he turns around one last time and says: "You're a brave guy, and this time it worked out. You found the entrance on your own and came all the way down here, but I wouldn't recommend getting lost down here to just anyone, so if you have any friends who want to visit the *bottini*, the only way to do so is to reserve a visit through the City in small groups (+39 0577 292614); and don't bring your cell phones, because photographs are prohibited." Then, just as he had appeared, he vanished.

As I start my ascent towards the surface, I find a brochure in my pocket that I had been looking for. It illustrates the **Museo dell'Acqua** (**Museum of Water** – www.museoacqua.comune.siena.it) at the **Fonti di Pescaia**: since 2010 this space offers a multimedia tour, through films, narrations and a section dedicated entirely to testaments from older citizens of the city. I would have liked to stop there had it not gotten so late. I take the last few steps along the stairway that leads me to the exit and the fresh scent of the air hits me and restores me: it's already evening, but not nearly as dark as the *bottini*.

Dotting the vault of the sky is a myriad of stars that seems to be waiting for me; before ending my day, I had a last wish, a last discovery to make. The legend of Saint Lawrence's tears never seemed to make much sense to me, and I've always been curious to find out more, yet in a more scientific way, with planets and constellations. In the past I had taken part of one of the evenings organized by the **Unione Astrofili Senesi (Union of Sienese Amateur Astronomists –** www.astrofilisenesi.it): with the help of telescopes and binoculars, the stars are our guide to the city at the *Specola Palmiero Capannoli* astronomy center in Via Laterino, at the *Osservatorio astronomico* at Porta Romana or, just a few kilometers outside of Siena, at the **Castello di Montarrenti**.

Dreams and reality walk hand in hand here: nighttime and silence have arrived. The street below me and the starry sky above me keep me company, who knows what new adventure awaits me tomorrow! I turn around, and the profile of Siena takes my breath way.

Chapter 9 / The Athlete

All in One Breath

Sprinting through sports in the city

I'm not the sedentary type, not one bit. I love moving, visiting the world on foot and, thanks to my muscles, not from behind a desk. When I arrived here everything around me was conveying tranquility. The exact opposite of the competitive quickness of an athletic movement: Siena seemed like a lady of old Roman aristocracy, sprawled on a chaise lounge. Instead, looking more closely, I discovered that behind those curtains there is a sprinter on the starting blocks. There, that's what Siena is to me. Sweet and tense, soave and irascible, all at the same time. Just like her streets.

After the slight downward slope of Piazza del Campo, one morning I got up the nerve to continue down **Via Duprè**. Not wanting to lose my concentration, I avoided stopping to see the astonishing view from the Piazza del Mercato towards Monte Amiata. The steep slope didn't scare me: I've always had good lungs. I must admit, though, that the hills in this town are no joke. Nevertheless, if you have the patience and the breath, your efforts will pay off. At the top of this hill in **Via Sant'Agata** is one of the most symbolic places for sports in the *Bel Paese*, especially considering its history with basketball.

Siena is a pioneer of sports: the *Mens Sana in Corpore Sano* Association was founded by a handful of *avantgarde* students in 1871. Not only did it reach huge numbers of members by the beginning of the 20th century, it saw the birth of fencing, track-and-field, running and cycling. Here basketball takes root in a capillary way, endemic, and much of its merit goes to that place that we see at the top of this street, after passing under a small arch that marks halfway up the hill. That's where I'm headed, because in that courtyard a game of basketball was played for the first time in Italy. At the time it was called *palla al cerchio*, ball in a circle, as this discipline was initially defined. The elegant aroma that you detect in the air is coming from the woman that was behind everything, the teacher **Ida Nomi Venerosi Pesciolini**. Born in Siena on September 1, 1873, she was a true ambassador of sports and culture, and was the first person to fall in love with this new team sport. The rules of the game pretty much fell into her hands and, immediately after reading and translating the 13 fundamental rules laid out by the inventor of the game, Mr. Naimsmith in person, decided the sport was fitting for her female students.

She immediately got to work and organized a demonstration to introduce basketball to the city. April 27, 1907 at 9 o'clock in the evening. The guests enter from the gate that is part of a break in the city walls and opens up into the courtyard, where a fanfare from the Association is ready to welcome the athletes. Today this place is almost unrecognizable, as it is now a university cafeteria, but the outside is pretty much the same and there, in the open air, they continued to play for many years, in the shadow of the gigantic building of the **Convitto Tolomei**, the classrooms of the city's Liceo Classico (Classics High School). This exhibition was held right in the gym of this courtyard, with one small setback: the crowd was too big, the stands overflowing, and more than once they had to lower the ropes to let everyone pass. Siena was anxious to see, so Maestra Nomi Pesciolini's young students were forced to reduce their playing field, at the time 14 x 7 meters (half of today's regulation size). It definitely wasn't a "regular" game but was more than enough for the Sienese: they had already fallen in love.

There is now a monument to this magical place where this first basketball match occurred, not by a simple sign, but by a painted key, right where the original basketball court arose, tread on by the precursors of this sport.

The most incredible thing is that, at the same time this was all happening, just a few hundred meters away, something else was coming into existence that would have strengthened Siena's roots in basketball. Let's move to yet another hill in Siena. We've passed through the **Fosso di Sant'Ansano**, with the Santa Maria della Scala imposing above us, and are headed towards the Ricreatorio Pio II, a place known in Siena as the **Costone**, nestled between the Fontebanda valley and the Duomo's hill. In 1907, enlightened priest **Don Nazareno Orlandi** was struck by this place's recreative potential and decided to found one of the most historical sports clubs in the city. Right away the Costone became, for so many children, a place for growing, playing, spending time together and living.

Hearing about Monsignor Orlandi will put a smile on your face. Born to a modest family in 1871, at a young age it was obvious he was destined to priesthood and teaching. Taking care of young people, helping them to mature in an environment that used games and sports as examples of Christian values: these were his amiable obsessions. In that space, bought for just 20.000 lire (today 10 euros) thanks to contributions and pledges that Orlando himself procured, he finally had the chance to move forward with his educational vision. This large area that looks out onto the San Prospero neighborhood was equipped with tennis and basketball courts, and even a swimming pool for a short period. Not just sports, though: the Costone, even today, boasts a small theater (⬥ www.costone.it) that has given many young actors, amateur and not, the chance to experience the thrill of being on stage for the first time. Today there is also a "relaxation" area, called *Gli Orti*, a green corner in the heart of Siena, surrounded by aromatic herbs and rose bushes. The basketball court is still there, still used often in the winter, but now its protagonists are rosemary, sage, marjoram and various fruit trees. Once past the entrance you may feel like you're in the middle of the countryside, a path leads past the court to a small chapel where Monsignor Orlandi is buried. As I leave, reinvigorated by the wholesome air in the chapel, I'm sure that, when it comes to basketball in Siena, everything that comes afterwards began in these two places: the intuitions of another priest and teacher, **Don Perucatti**, who founds the third basketball association in Siena, **Virtus**, to the victories of the Mens Sana in the recent past. The life of basketball in this city, although seemingly in decline, will always have a solid foundation from which to kick back off.

My walk continues, I'm still not out of breath. After going uphill, I'm dying to run down one of the craziest hills in the city, bringing me to the **fonti di Fontebranda**, where there was once a public swimming pool, set up to offer the Sienese a revitalizing swim. I reach the bottom, attracted by the sound of running water, but in the blink of an eye I'm going back up! This city is like the tracks of a roller coaster, putting my endurance (and calves!) to the test. At the top of this hill I climb the last few steps; the view of Siena is breathtaking and the majestic shadow of the Basilica of San Domenico gives me a second to catch my breath. Breath that so many runners who have passed me up seem to have, all direct to the place in which, among sycamores and oaks, everyone in Siena goes to run: the path above the **Fortezza Medicea**.

Sure, professionals prefer the new track at the **Campo Scuola in Viale Avignone**, but I'm interested in the Fortezza, where the amateur runner can relish in the views of the countryside and admire the city at the same time, all within the same running loop. Peace and tranquility, hearing nothing more than the sound of their own feet and breath.

The passion for running is becoming more and more alive around here; so many events are organized in and around the city. A few stand out: the **Ultramarathon Terre di Siena** (⟲ www.terredisienaultra-marathon.it) and the **Ecomaratona del Chianti Classico** (⟲ www.ecomaratonadelchianticlassico.it), in which love for this sport and postcard landscapes unite. Today runners and walkers, yesterday meeting place for other athletic events: in fact, many equestrian competitions have been held in the fortress (paling in comparison to the Palio, obviously…), as well as a famous boxing match that was once organized in the central area, boasting Primo Carnera, king of Italian boxing, as its protagonist.

From the fortress, originally created by the Emperor Charles V as a fortified citadel and then rebuilt by Cosimo I Medici after the fall of the Republic of Siena, not only can you marvel at the beauty of the city, but you also get a great view of anther symbol of this area, the stadium, dedicated to a Sienese that made Italian soccer history, **Artemio Franchi**, later nicknamed "**il Rastrello**" (**the rake**). Years before (at the beginning of the 1920's), that space that connected San Propsero to the center of the city was just a dusty area where the Robur, historical city team, often trained. The project to turn that valley into a place for soccer fans (but not just) to meet up, equipped with a central field and stands that would be able to hold more than 20,000 people began shortly after. Things took much longer than what was originally planned, and in 1938 the stadium was finished. From then on, every Sunday, that natural hollow has welcomed the Sienese, passionate about their black and white colors. I did mention that it's not just soccer. At the Rastrello, on the track that surrounds the grassy field, bicycles have passed, sprinters have soared, engines have roared (the Sienese may want to tell you about a motorcycle race with pilot Giacomo Agostini that ended right here…could it be true?). In 1979, during the last Meeting dell'Amicizia organized in Italy ("Friendly Meeting" - a national track and field event held in Siena), another champion, sprinter **Pietro Mennea**, shocked spectators with his gazelle-like legs.

I keep going, I've still got some breath left in me. This time I decide to take a **bicycle** available to the public by the City of Siena, among those stationed in the **San Prospero** neighborhood (the bike-sharing service, organized in 15 stations across the city, works with a small fee - 10 euros for 24 hours. The app is available here: 🔗 www.comune.siena.it). I cross the Lizza park and head towards Fonte Giusta; I move coasting the walls and the famous **Fortino delle Donne** (**Women's Fortress**), erected by noble Sienese women during the

Spanish siege, and symbol of the Republic of Siena's resistance. I turn left near **Porta Camollia**, whose inscription on the stones reads: *Cor magis tibi sena pandit* (Siena opens a larger heart to you [larger than the gate you are crossing]), it reminds me of the culture of hospitality that runs in the blood of this city.

I've got the sudden urge to take a swim. In the nearby **Piazza Amendola** is the smaller of two **public swimming pools** in Siena. The other is a bit farther away, in the **Acqua Calda** neighborhood. Nonetheless, since I'm already nearby, I can't not check out the other Sienese athletic facilities. The first one is the **rugby field**, baptized *il sabbione*, **the big sand box**, for the total absence of grass since its construction: a portion of the Sahara transported to the Siena suburbs. You can imagine the conditions of the terrain after just a few drops of rain: a unique, enormous quicksand. Despite this, if you get close to the net surrounding the field, you can still hear the epic yells of the matches of one of the noblest of team sports. Every match, peppered with blows and punches of all kinds, ends with a final toast at the center of the field, with a flask of Chianti (the English will forgive this "transgression") that unites the two teams. I like it: maybe I'll start playing rugby.

Speaking of noble sports, over there I notice a round building, inside which some of the most important Italian fencers have practiced, and who have made the Sienese school one of the most renowned in Italy, with champions such as **Margherita Zalaffi** (gold medalist at the Barcelona Olympics in 1992). This is the **CUS facility** that, more than just a springboard for fencing, hosts basketball and volleyball teams at the university level and that later became an attractive center for many young people in the city. This area definitely isn't as fascinating as the poetic streets of the historical center, but it bleeds sports in all senses, and that's what I'm looking for on my long tour around town. In this area we can find two more facilities for cycling lovers: the velodrome and the new **Anne Frank park**, a bike park outfitted with jumps and ditches for off-road and mountain bikes.

Heading back to the center of the city, I follow the directions for the train station and, before getting there, I see two small sports buildings on my left: the legendary **Dodecaedro**, a twelve-sided psychedelic building where epic battles down to the last basket have been fought, and the more modern **PalaEstra**, seat of the Mens Sana's Polisportiva, where many other sports are practiced, from basketball to handball to volleyball. **Emma Villas Volley's** training is famous because, after having "fought" in the national championship, it has favored important initiatives, such as the return of the national volleyball championships after many years. That building isn't just courts and stands, as I enter I notice that, in the belly of this place, there are many rooms where, with patience and dedication, talents in artistic gymnastics, skating and other disciplines can flourish. Places that breathe high-quality sports 24 hours a day.

I continue and turn right, where the next hill awaits me, but this time my two-wheeled, motor assist bicycle comes to my assistance. I leave the bike in Via Vittorio Emanuele, at the **Antiporto** bike station (a medieval fortification constructed to better protect the entrance to the city from the north) and go on by foot, through the Porta Camollia. I run towards Piazza del Campo, but this time I cut through Via della Stufa Secca, where they told me there is a place tied to a legendary personality of Sienese sports. The master **Bargaglio**, one of the first fencers in Italy to open a prestigious school for future swordsmen and foilsmen.

I'm finally in Piazza del Campo, one of the most beautiful *piazze* in the world. I'm really starting to get short of breath, but before finishing my run, I have a couple more important stops: I'll use the air that's left in my lungs to enjoy a great dinner before some well-deserved rest.

THE ANTIQUE SPIRIT OF CYCLING

One day I felt the need to move my legs in a different way. I let my feet get some rest, but this certainly doesn't mean that I stopped moving. I simply put them in the pedals of a bicycle, adventuring out to discover the infinite countryside paths that surround Siena. All around, a varied, colorful, surprising landscape. I was purposely trying to lose myself, to let the hilly surroundings roll along together with my thoughts, wet with the sweat on my forehead.

Then I remembered that the province of Siena has in recent years become one of the most well-known settings for the world of cycling. Here, in 2008, one of the "great classic" cycling competitions was born, the **Strade Bianche** (www.strade-bianche.it), or white streets, a race whose name itself evokes images from other times, those of a cycling competition that felt like an epic voyage. Before I finished writing the word in Google, and all the information was already popping up, including a map of the itinerary. I would like to have the time to cover it all, slowly, in different legs, stopping at all the small towns along the way. Every year, in March, the professionals complete it in just over five hours, at a furious pace; "the most classic Northern race in Southern Europe," they call it.

I appreciate how the organizers unite certain portions of difficult, uneven streets typical of the Paris-Roubaix race, with sudden changes of slope just like another great classic, the Tour of Flanders. I have no reason to do it all in one sweep, like they do: I can take my time as a bicycle tourist. The itinerary changes every year; in the first years they used the **Chianti hills** as a backdrop; one year the start was set in **San Gimignano**, another gem worth admiring in this treasured province; the most recent editions, rather, have explored sections south of the city, with a leg circling through **Buonconvento**, **Montalcino** and the magical **Crete Senesi**.

If that wasn't enough for this place, in 1997 another idea took shape that satisfied the lovers of cycling. They called it the **Eroica, a heroic race**. In practice, it's another occasion to revoke and bring alive the old spirits of cycling. It's not a true race, technically it's a "bicycle tourism ride," but attracts over 7,000 participants from all over the world, all abiding by a strict set of rules, most importantly bikes and apparel that must be rigorously vintage (some ride on models from the early

20th century). Want to save the date? It's the first Sunday of October in **Gaiole in Chianti** (www.eroica.cc).

My initial intention of getting lost among these streets has already jumped ship: I'm just not the type for picnics and all-round relaxation. I want to choose one of these paths, but not to try to challenge the champions. I want to, as I love to do, challenge myself and my abilities.

I've already said enough, my legs are shaking, I've just got to choose the right path.

Chapter 10 / The Night Owl

When the Night is Young

For the trendiest

Ten sounds pretty good: it's my number, the number of the stars. And in this chapter you will feel just like one! Let's start with the alarm, it goes off late in the morning…A quick look in the mirror and I ask myself a question to figure out what mood I'm in: do we feel more classic or more rock? You know, it's good to change styles, that way you never get bored. What do you suggest for the big night ahead of us? What will best help us conquer Siena? You know what, it's the perfect day to double up and choose both. At least for today, since it's my birthday…

#FiveStarLunch

Let's start off with a more classic look. In Siena, if the night is young and the day starts in the early afternoon, the best choice is a good brunch with friends at **Te Ke Voi** (Vicolo di San Pietro, +39 0577 40139) or the **San Paolo Pub** (Vicolo di San Paolo, +39 0577 564321), two perfect places for all seasons and all ages. With just a few bucks, in both places you can have a good pizza or an overflowing sandwich, maybe choosing to sit outside, as they both have tables set up under the arches of the alleys. At San Paolo the outside balcony is the coolest place on a sunny day, looking out onto Piazza del Campo. Sports fans can even take a quick glance at NBA games or soccer matches, for a truly "fast" lunch.

Or do we want to be less conventional? Let's get takeaway. The **Pizzeria Poppi,** in Via Banchi di Sotto 25 (📞 +39 0577 40207), is a must, with its tasty sliced pizza.

But the true specialty not to miss is Poppi's famous *ciaccino. Ciaccino* in Siena is a kind of *focaccia,* usually filled with mozzarella and *prosciutto* or sausage. Even the mixed vegetable *ciaccino* makes my mouth water. The best part about Poppi is that it's tradition, everyone eats it, from kids to grandparents; you can have it for lunch or a hearty snack. Another characteristic of this place is that you eat standing, quick and without too many frills. If it's a nice day, you can enjoy your ciaccino in Piazza del Campo, just head down **Vicolo dei Borsellai** and you're already there. I've eaten my fair share leaning against the column at the entrance to the *vicolo.*

Heading further down Via di Pantaneto, **Pastazuf** (🔗 www. pastazuf.it, the Osteria Babazuf's lunch-time only brother next door), gives you a nice plate of homemade pasta, as well as finger foods or second courses you can enjoy at the few tables inside (outdoor seating available in the summer) or even to go.

Down the road is **Meet Life Cafè** (📞 +39 0577 270258), a place I recommend for a lazy afternoon of chatting in the booths, watching the game, maybe sipping a beer or a good coffee (they offer a great variety). For an *aperitivo,* Wednesday evenings the place transforms into an open gallery for young artists and wine tastings.

#ÀlaMode

"Guys, what are we going to do from now until dinner?" I hear someone ask. There's just enough time to enjoy some sun and take a look at the best stores in town: some new clothes are exactly what I need, for a touch of class to flaunt tonight…just to make some of those old friends that I haven't seen in a while jealous.

Franchi (📞 +39 0577 40015), in Via Banchi di Sopra, also known as the Corso, are the first windows to check out.

At number 51, this two-story space is ideal for the most fashionable shoes, shirts and pants. Its layout is inviting, among digital projections, crystal lamps from the 1970s and musical instruments or bicycles hanging from the walls.

One of Siena's historical brands is **Cortecci** (www.corteccisiena.it) on the corner of Piazza del Campo and Costarella dei Barbieri. Its style is classic and timeless. If you're looking for a suit I would recommend trying **Grey** in Via dei Montanini (+39 0577 287785), then complete your outfit at the **Cravattificio di Siena** (www.cravattificiosiena.com) in front of the Battistero di San Giovanni, with a bowtie or a soft, short, perfectly fashionable tie.

Otherwise, most young men prefer **Scout** (+39 0577 223474) in Via dei Montanini, with its trendy combinations of jeans and t-shirts.

Some good suggestions for women's clothing? **Futuro's** in Via dei Montanini (+39 0577 281080) is a boutique for those who love colors and accessories from mixed brands; **Mag Boutique** (www.magboutique.it), is a sought out place with excellent ideas for an original touch to your wardrobe; **Dolci Trame** (www.dolcitrame.store) in its "living room" in Via di Pantaneto, is a unique brand with a touch of class and elegance.

Looking for more?

A last look down this street, there's so much to choose from: take a trip into **Baraka e Ziggy** (+39 0577 247404) for clothing at a good price, and its neighbors **Corsini** (www.corsinico2.it) and **Degortes** (www.degortes.net), with more brand-name men's and women's apparel.

After doing some shopping "for her" let's catch our breath with some men's fashion in Via di Calzoleria, where in just a few meters we pass from the classic **Accordi** (www.accordi-abbigliamento.business.site) to the eccentric and young **Kaotik** (www.kaotik.shop).

If you would rather shop vintage, go to the nearby Via del Porrione, where you can find the legendary **Aloe&Wolf** (www.aloewolf.it). As extravagant as can be, it's a corner where you can discover collections from other times: lamps, jewelry, vintage accessories, magazines. But most of all clothes chosen directly by Alessandra, the passionate owner who often livens up the shop with exhibits, fashion shows and aperitifs. The most fashionable will have heard of "Swinging on Porrione," one of the most glamourous events of the city, that every once in a while makes the thirties come alive again on this street, with live swing music, street food and Lindy hop dancers.

Since we're already in the neighborhood, last but not least and right in front of Aloe&Wof, is **Tutte 'ose** (📞 +39 0577 226677), which deserves a thorough look through. A cute shop where, true to its name (which means all things), you can really find anything, like a needle in a haystack: ideal for home decor items, but also for stocking up on gift ideas.

"But don't you want to make a quick stop and go at some international brands?" Your tireless lady friend will surely ask. Let's be honest, we men have enough of shopping at a certain point…and so you'll have to compromise: "Let's go there tomorrow for your birthday!" On the other hand, the big brands can be found every day in the big cities, so for one day they can be set aside, no?

#FeelingMyBest

The most important part of the evening - we'll all agree - has to be the accessories, if you really want to be a part of the night owl club: it's here that you recognize true glamour. Search out the corner of Piazza Tolomei and Via Cecco Angiolieri, and you'll find a small store with big charm. **Momi** (📞 +39 347 2747124) is a concentration of details and passion from the moment you walk into the door. Need something to boost your mood? Walk inside this small store and you'll feel at home.

The hats are all high quality, the name Borsalino hangs in the air. Some advice? Try one on in the mirror and it'll make you feel like Humphrey Bogart from *Casablanca*.

If you're looking for something more historical, try the **Cappelleria Terzi** in Via Banchi di Sotto 29 (📞 +39 0577 270324). You'll feel yourself suddenly thrown into a jazz jam session that you can be a part of…try on and choose your favorite hat by looking in one of the two liberty mirrors from the beginning of the 20th century. There's something for everyone: from a wide-brimmed Panizza to a Coppola style, or maybe a beret; you can even find a goliardo, typical gear for the *Feriae Matricularum Senensium* celebrations, several days of festivities in May for Sienese male university students. Hats off to Stefano, who is keeping the family's tradition alive. A true classic that began in Piazza del Campo in 1850.

The **Cappelleria Bertacchi** (www.cappelleriabertacchi.com) in Via di Città 60 is much younger and more rock and roll: simple style, reasonable prices, sharp and full of colorful shelves. It recently made news when the Obama family visited Siena in May 2017: photographers and passersby witnessed the charismatic Michelle come out of this store with a big white Panama hat on her head.

If you're still with your friend, maybe it's time to check out some purses? You'll make her happy at the **Pelletteria Falchini**, one of the most famous brands in Tuscany (the store in Siena opened in 1931), with a history that spans three generations (www.pelletteriafalchini.com). This female-run store offers the best brand-name selection of purses and luggage in its two locations in Via Banchi di Sotto and, outside of the center, in Strada Massetana Romana.

Keeping with the leather theme, you must stop in to **Cardinali** (+39 0577 272432), with its two locations both in Via Banchi di Sotto. The more welcoming one is at number 50, but don't underestimate the younger look of the one at number 16, which offers everything from sweaters to shoes to accessories.

If you're looking for a pair of sunglasses, another well-known Sienese shop in Banchi di Sotto is **Ottica Ricci** (www.otticaricci.it), inside the 14th century Palazzo Sansedoni since 1951. In recent years, its remodeling has transformed it into one of the coolest spaces in the city center, where both Sienese and tourists alike can appreciate its quality and professionalism (as well as its other two locations in Banchi di Sopra and Strada Massetana Romana).

Let's stop to think for a minute…maybe even less since I've already decided what whim to satisfy next. Yes, a good cigar is exactly what I need for the night ahead. **Il Chiasso Largo** in Via Rinaldini (+39 0577 282162) has, without a doubt, one of the best selections in town. Luca can recommend the right aromas for you. There is a lot to choose from, even though I'm dead set on a pure Cuban, just to make the night special. Now, though, it's time to unwind. It's time for my favorite part of the day: happy hour.

#HappyHour

In the category "classic relaxation" is **Morbidi** (www.morbidi.com), in Banchi di Sopra. Not only is it an excellent (and historic) deli for your daily lunch break, but a welcoming and elegant place. Often crowded on the weekend, the long bar at the entrance is well known for its display of high quality buffet. There's no table service: you eat standing up or sitting on the stools at the bar, or as I like to, right in the middle of everyone.

Another lively place is **Bar La Favorita** (+39 0577 41932), in Piazza Matteotti, the first one you come to after parking in one of the most convenient places, the Stadium (free in the evenings). **Caveau Dinner Club** is in the spaces below, with a separate entrance from Viale Tozzi, and has the same management. First try the *aperitivi*, then watch as the place transforms into a dance floor.

Is this the right night for opening a special bottle? The **Bottiglieria Salefino** (+39 0577 44685) in Piazza del Sale, on the other side of the restaurant with the same name, offers a quiet corner for relaxing over a classy wine and food pairing (oysters are always on the menu!). Claudio and Alice have created a novel greenhouse inside with an elegant and romantic touch. There are delicious corners where you can pass pleasant hours indoors or, when the temperatures allow, enjoy the welcoming outdoor space with its marble benches.

If you're looking for a more artistic atmosphere in a timeless courtyard, the Palazzo Chigi Saracini's **ChigianArtCafé** (www.chigiana.org/chigianartcafe), where its outdoor tables surrounding an ancient well are ideal for sipping a drink and listening to some live music, coming directly from the Chigiana Music Academy.

Another trendy spot is **Tre Filari** (www.trefilari.it), on the corner of Via Banchi di Sotto and Via San Vigilio. A refined wine bar, with its bottles on display and a wide, yet always crowded bar. It's pleasant drinking an aperitivo even outside, leaning against the wooden shelves. The large wine selection is a protagonist here along with the *alzate*, a selection of local products.

If we're feeling more like a star, there's no better stage than Piazza del Campo: behind Fonte Gaia and directly facing the Palazzo Pubblico, **Bar Il Palio** (📞 +39 0577 282055) is one of the most frequented year round by Sienese, with its outdoor tables (heated in the winter), from which you can greet friends and observe passersby stopping in the Piazza's slice near the San Martino curve (especially during the Palio days). Next up are **Bar Manganelli** (📞 +39 0577 284071) and the **Gran Caffè Siena** part of the Nannini franchise (📞 +39 0577 284424), under new management, and for many years called La Birreria. Both places are excellent choices for a quick drink, or slowly sipping a cocktail, looking out onto the Piazza. At Bar Manganelli I usually grab a quick drink at the bar; at the Gran Caffè Siena the atmosphere's a bit more relaxed, with music, tables and a television.

There are so many other streets to explore if we wanted to be more "alternative." When I'm looking for a local student bar, **Caffetteria Diacceto** (📞 +39 333 9385763) is ideal, with its outdoor tables just a few meters from Piazza Indipendenza. Simple and cheap, a bit hidden from view, but always filled with young people who don't mind sitting in the street, the window with newspapers to browse and the nearby "romantic" view of San Domenico as the street begins to climb towards the Battistero di San Giovanni.

Or do we want to snob the center for now, since we'll be coming back later? We can easily get to **Dream Café** and **Al Fiumino** by car, both in strategic positions for anyone coming from Siena Nord. On main streets and with ample parking, they are welcoming and popular, great meeting points from any place near the city. They definitely don't look onto Piazza del Campo, but **Dream Café** (📞 +39 347 8025428) has a large outdoor terrace truly enjoyable in all seasons. **Al Fiumino** (📞 +39 0577 892065), on the other hand, is at a gas station. But don't let appearances deceive you, because it's "truck stop style" can have a certain appeal, and the food is top quality.

What should we get? Are you up for classic cocktails (in Siena the *Conca d'oro* used to be popular), or do you like experimenting the more modern Moscow Mule, Hugo or *Negroni sbagliato* (the gin is replaced by spumante)? I'll go with something classic, a *spritz*. There's always time to step it up…

#DinnerTime

Rule number one: if the night is young, never eat dinner before 10 p.m.! But remember, if you follow this trend, make sure to make reservations because Siena isn't New York and you'll risk not finding a table and getting stuck with catching a quick meal off the street. Well, our first choice has always and will always be Piazza del Campo: sitting in the city's living room has its charm. My favorite "slice" of Piazza del Campo is the closest one to the San Martino curve, where I can sit outdoors at the **Osteria del Bigelli** (📞 +39 0577 1511456) and the **Bandierino** (🔗 www.ristoranteilbandierino-siena.com). Otherwise, on the other side, you can oversee the piazza from **Osteria La Mossa** (📞 +39 0577 40989), a small restaurant adjacent to the Costarella entrance.

A paradise for tranquility and class is the new **Battistero Bistrot** (🔗 www.battisterosiena.com/bistrot), situated in the center of Piazza San Giovanni. In front of the monumental Baptistery (from which it takes its name), the outdoor tables, which are heated in the winter, are popular at all hours, from breakfast to dinner. Yet it's the aperitivo/dinner hour that we can enjoy the best atmosphere here, among cocktails, wine and unforgettable dishes.

Other popular places? Move over to San Domenico, where Il **Pomodorino** (🔗 www.ilpomodorino.it) and **Nonno Mede** (📞 +39 0577 247966), with pizza and Tuscan cooking (respectively) will know how to satisfy your romantic side, with their views on the Duomo and the Torre del Mangia.

But the coolest street for our dinner (and after) is **Via di Pantaneo**, that is crawling in night life from lunch on: university students are in the majority here, but also other young adults and tourists can be found here, looking for meals at all hours.

Down at number 89, a place you don't want to miss is **La Prosciutteria Crudi e Bollicine** (🔗 www.laprosciutteria.com/aperitivo-siena) that welcomes us with its finely decorated rooms, in a labyrinth of coves in its unique fashion (its wood-paneled wall in the elegant room which faces a large external window are worth the price of the evening). Tartars and *carpacci* are the menu's protagonists, but it's the contagious charm of those who work here that create the perfect atmosphere for our meal. On summer weekends the outdoor tables set along the street are perfect for enjoying the evening without having to worry about passing traffic.

Looking to quench your thirst with some beer? You don't have to go very far, **Birra Bader** (www.birrabader.it) is down at number 75. An antiquely furnished space that makes use of the old Sienese beer making tradition from the late 1800s, originally opened by Guglielmo Bader according to the "German method." Now you can taste white, lightly fermented beer, a pleasant treat for all palates, accompanied by sandwiches, *ciaccini* (Sienese focaccia) and other light Tuscan dishes.

Still not full? Move over to the **Fabbrica Bader** (www.fabbricabader.com) in Vicolo della Manna, just a few meters from Piazza del Campo, where there is "house beer" and a notably long list of "all colors" of Spritz cocktails. The menu boasts typical Sienese dishes, charcuterie boards with cold cuts and cheese, but also vegetarian flan and exquisite creamy baccalà.

#Drinks&Music

Dear people of the night, who doesn't like a little bit of music?

And so we enter into **Bottega Roots Siena** (+39 0577 892482) in Via di Pantaneto, a vintage style bistro that has the right feel for a good glass of wine. "Soul food for music lovers" is the place's spot-on slogan, for a cocktail bar that brings to life both the spirit of Sonar, the music house in Colle Val d'Elsa and the sensibility of The B. Side Association for its live music, in this surprising blend of art and gourmet restoration.

Are you crazy about jazz? You have to go to the Salicotto neighborhood and sit at a table at **Un Tubo** (www.untubo.com), in the characteristic Via del Luparello. A perfect den for artists of the Accademia Nazionale del Jazz (National Jazz Academy) and Miles Davis and Bill Evans fans, the quality of the concerts held here are guaranteed by its collaboration with Siena Jazz and the Scuola Ronaldo Franci (local institute of musical studies). Its wine cellar is without a doubt top notch: more than 1,200 quality labels kept in the rooms dug in the sandstone during the 15th century. The wine selection is fruit of the painstaking work and passion of Gianni and Laura Brunelli, owners of the nearby and famous **Osteria Le Logge** (📶 www.osterialelogge.it). Its kitchen, visible from the street, is among the most beautiful in Siena, worthy of a movie set; but not less than its wine menu, shared with the more intimate Tubo. If you're feeling *Kind of Blue*, look for its jazz nights. They are usually on Fridays, but the program changes often: otherwise, what kind of "improvisation" would it be?

Another place to keep in mind is **I Parolai** (📶 www.iparolai.it), right outside Porta Ovile. Born as a tapas bar, if offers more Italian versions of tapas and delicious cocktails (generally strong, I have a weak side for the *Sbagliatissimo*, with vermouth and aged *millesimato* spumante from Felsina, excellent Chianti Classico wine maker). The added value of being at I Parolai is a great mix of taste and sound, with the possibility of choosing between the two floors of the bar and the covered outdoor seating. On Wednesdays they often hold wine tastings from Zero KM producers, accompanied by some acoustic duos; on Fridays they host live music.

Let's change *genre*. If you're not looking for music to be the highlight of the night, but rather in the background, for your after aperitif or after dinner drinks, the heart of the movida in Siena is still around the Logge del Papa and Via di Pantaneto, bordering Piazza del Campo. There you'll just have to lend an ear to hear where the people are gathering. **Caffè Le Logge** (📞 +39 349 3530968) is just the right amount of original, with a clientele that I would call bohemian: glass in hand, standing next to the bar, sitting at the tables of the elegant loft, or in the street hanging out with friends.

It's impossible not to notice the nearby bar and panino shop **Bibò** (📞 +39 0577 44608): right in front there's usually groups of young students. You might even have a hard time getting through the street because this bar is famous for its low prices and the possibility of chatting on the steps on the opposite Palazzo Piccolomini.

Moving over a bit, Via del Porrione is another street that is crawling with young people having a good time at **Cor Magis** (📞 +39 0577 43182) and **Bar Porrione** (📞 +39 0577 43295): two neighbors with tables on the street, crowded in the evening with people just a few steps away from the Torre del Mangia and a view of the famous San Marino curve.

#DancingAllNight

Here's my recommendations for the rowdier crowd. If you want to go dancing in the city, check out the historical **Al Cambio** (📞 +39 0577 43183, Via di Pantaneto 48). Typically underground, it's known for its Disco Saturdays, but doesn't turn its nose up to live music on the other days of the week (especially for university nights on Thursdays). Here, some will remember, the rock band from Arezzo, Negrita, had some of its first shows. Destination for the youngest, this up close and personal with musicians is its greatest attraction, because there's no distance between you and the band. An important reminder: mind the step! The step at the entrance to the place, the one that leads you to the long corridor that hugs the bar, has had more victims that the Black Plague in 1348…

A classic that never goes out of fashion is the **Corte dei Miracoli** (🔗 www.lacortedeimiracoli.org), a cultural association and social non-profit in Via Roma, part of the complex of the San Niccolò ex-psychiatric hospital. Different languages walk hand in hand here: not just music and concerts, but also art shows, book presentations, theatre and dance, for a good kind of "contamination" of culture and genres.

Right outside of the city you can go dancing at the **Vanilla Disco Club** (✉ vanilladiscosiena@gmail.com) in Pian del Casone, near Monteriggioni, maybe making a stop on the way at the **Bar dell'Orso** (🔗 www.ilbardellorso.it), right there at the Colonna di Monteriggioni, and order a big tray of Tuscan cold cuts and cheese before getting out on the floor.

Papillon 78 (📶 www.papillon78.it) in Monteroni d'Arbia is in the opposite direction, that since 1978 has been organizing Saturday nights and is open until four o'clock in the morning. Going there and back with the free shuttle from Piazza Gramsci is the best (two shuttles run each way, each an hour from each other), no worries about driving and the night takes on a whole new meaning…

#OffToBed

For anyone still in town, there's always someone in Piazza del Campo until late, sitting on the fish bone bricks, or leaning on its famous columns. If you've worked up an appetite, go to the Hamburger and Steakhouse in Via Pantaneto, **Al Volo** (📶 www.alvolosiena.com), where you can make your own late-night panino. To quench your thirst, the last pit stop you should make in the city is **Caffè del Corso** in via Banchi di Sopra (📞 +39 0577 226656), in a strategic position on your way back to where you parked at the Stadium, and where you'll meet the professional night owls.

In Via della Sapienza (near San Domenico's Basilica), on weekends until 2 a.m. you can find groups of young adults waiting for their last bite of the night at the **Paninoteca Da Poldo** (📶 www.dapoldo.it): a great choice for *piadina* lovers or hamburgers made in the American fashion, served with fries and any and all combinations of sauces. The extra advantage here is filling up with just a few euros.

Now that the night is over and dawn is coming, I'm in the mood for a *caramellato* at the **Pasticceria Buti** to end my night on a sweet note, or rather, start my day with a "breakfast for champions." You've never tasted one? It's a cream-filled pastry with a crunchy caramelized outer layer and garnished in white chocolate. There are usually two options: maybe you've foreseen your appetite for these the night before and stocked up with a tray for the whole family. If not, no panic, right outside Porta Camollia, in Viale Vittorio Emanuele II, the **Pasticceria Buti** (📶 www.pasticceriabuti.it) opens its doors at 7a.m. (remember: at 8a.m. on Sundays, and is closed on Mondays).

You'll just need to watch the clock for a bit while you wait for this well-deserved "heavenly meal." Is or isn't it my birthday?

Oops, at least it was! Good night, everyone, it's not every night we get to live like this!

P.S.: I almost forgot, dear night owl friends…If you happen in Siena in the summer, don't miss out on any of the *feste titolari* organized within each specific *contrada* for at least a week, lively evenings in honor of their respective Patron Saint. The *Valdimontone* opens the season with theirs at the end of April, while the *Aquila* closes it out around mid-September. You'll hear of the "Pania" in the *Nicchio*, the "Oliveta" for the *Chiocciola*, the "Mangia e Bevi" in the *Torre* and even about the "Baobello Chef" in the *Bruco's* garden. Depending on the season, try them all!

They are not only tasty (for those with a hearty appetite) but fun (for those who want to dance into the night). They are almost always set in the most beautiful gardens and outdoor areas of the city for those who want to enjoy the views from within the walls accompanied by music, tradition and good Tuscan cuisine.

Enjoy!

Useful Information for the Perfect Planner

Siena

Region: Tuscany
Province: Siena (SI)
Zip code: 53100
Population: approx. 54,000
Prefix: +39 0577
Coordinates: latitude 43.32018; longitude 11.33069

Patron Saint Feast Days:
- December 01: Saint Ansano
- April 29: Saint Catherine of Siena

Useful Numbers
- **Police station**, Via del Castoro 6, +39 0577 201111
- **Taxi**: +39 0577 49222
- **Parking**: Siena Parcheggi, Via S. Agata 1, +39 0577 228711
- **City Police**, Via F. Tozzi 3, +39 0577 292554
- **Bus**: Autolinee Toscane, info www.at-bus.it; Tiemme Toscana Mobilità, info www.tiemmespa.it/. **Ticket point Siena**: underground office in Piazza Gramsci and in train station entrance (Piazzale Rosselli)
- **Main Post Office**, Piazza Matteotti 37, +39 0577 214295
- **City of Siena Division of Tourism,** Piazza del Campo 1, +39 0577 292128/292178

Getting to Siena
- **By car**: the historical center is closed to traffic (except for public transportation and residents). The ZTL (limited traffic zone) is generally marked by the medieval walls and the entrances are equipped with video cameras connected directly to the offices of the City Police and active 24 hours a day. Here are the most convenient **parking garages** (you can check out the complete list here: www.sienaparcheggi.com). If you're coming from the North (Siena-Firenze highway): open **parking Stadio-Fortezza**, take the Siena Nord or Siena Acqua Calda exit, follow directions for the Stadio, the main entrance is in front of the Basilica di San Domenico and costs two euros per hour (€26 per day), but it is free at night (from 8pm-7am). Be careful, however, because on **Wednesdays** it's closed for the **open-air market** and for the Siena Robur home soccer games. If you're coming from the South (from Rome or Perugia, on the Siena-Bettolle highway): take the Siena Ovest exit, and head towards the covered parking called **Il Duomo**; otherwise, take the Siena Sud

exit for the covered parking called **Il Campo**. Both cost two euros per hour, or a total of €35 per day (price discounted to €25 if you're staying in a hotel in Siena). Other convenient parking with the same costs are **Santa Caterina** (Via Esterna di Fontebranda, South Siena) and **San Francesco** (Via Baldassarre Peruzzi, East Siena): they both have covered and uncovered parking and are just a few steps from the escalators that take you up into the center of the city. The most inexpensive covered parking is at the train station, **Stazione FS**: the first hour costs just €0.50 and then €2 for every hour afterwards.

– **Free parking** at the gates of the city: on one side of the Fortress, in Viale Vittorio Veneto is the Il **Campino parking**. A bit further on, in the San Prospero neighborhood, offers street parking in its maze-like streets and a small hidden parking area from Via Bonci.
If you're lucky you just might find some parking within the medieval walls. Entering in Porta Ovile there are several free parking spots in **Via Pian d'Ovile**. Same for Porta San Marco, passing through Porta Laterina, there are many along **Via Laterino**, close to the city cemetery. Otherwise, you can find white parking spots **along the external walls of the city**: outside Porta Camollia, in Via Don Giovanni Minzoni or Via Nino Bixio; outside Por-

ta Romana, in Via Girolamo Gigli or outside Porta Pispini, in Via Aretina. Just make sure to check the signs for which day of the week the street cleaners pass, just to avoid an unwanted ticket.

– **In the days of the Palio**, availability changes due to which *contrade* participate in the Palio, and it will be very difficult to park close to the center. You'll have better luck with the **commuter parking** on the edges of the city. There is a large one in Viale Toselli, n. 1973 (Due Ponti area) and another just as you get off the highway at the Acqua Calda exit (in front of a sports complex). Two more are in Massetana Romana, at the intersection with Strada dei Tufi, and at the Colonna San Marco. From there you can take the ***pollicino*** (little shuttle bus) that enters into the walls and within the ZTL.

– **By train**: the square in front of the train station, Piazzale Fratelli Rosselli is not within the walls, but very easily connected by the escalators, called the **Risalita Stazione-Antiporto-Porta Camollia**, open 24 hours a day. From the top of the escalators Piazza del Campo is a 15-minute stroll. Otherwise, from the station there are several urban bus lines that guarantee passage both to and from the center (Piazza del Sale) or to the hospital Santa Maria alle Scotte every 15 minutes.

– **For campers**: there are 95 total available posts for two specifically outfitted parking areas, with a daily cost of 20 euros. The **Fagiolone parking**, in Strada di Pescaia, is very convenient for its proximity to the historical center, it's a 20-minute walk from Via Esterna di Fontebranda to Piazza del Campo: the street is uphill, and if you're having a hard time, take the escalators you come across about half way up, which lead to Via Vallepiatta, right behind the Duomo. The other parking area, **Palasport**, is in Via Achille Sclavo, adjacent to the Mens Sana sports complex, and is the perfect solution for those looking for a more secluded area. In the North area of the city, the guaranteed bus lines 7 and 4 bring people directly to Piazza del Sale, or with the n. 9 you can reach the Fortress. You can even walk: in about 10 minutes you'll reach the train station, and from there take the escalators (see directions in the "by train" section).

– **By bus**: the busses to and from other Italian cities (most commonly Florence, Grosseto, Pisa, Rome, Milan) depart from the central Piazza Gramsci or the train station. Other urban busses stop in Piazza del Sale. Tickets are available at the main ticket office (in the underground area of La Lizza and Piazza Gramsci, or at the train station) or in authorized sellers (most newsstands or tabaccheria stores). Tickets can also be bought on board (for a higher price), by paying the driver directly. We recommend using the **Free App "AT bus"** and **"Tiemme Mobile"** to help you plan your trips, see real-time schedules, and acquire tickets with a click, by SMS.
More info here: www.at-bus.it; www.tiemmespa.it.

– **By motorcycle or scooter**: most of the ZTL area is accessible on two wheels. We recommend you enter the walls and park in the center of the city, to then move around on foot. The best parking in the North part of the city are at the **Basilica di San Domenico**, or the white parking spots at **La Lizza** and around the **stadium**. If you're coming from the south, then take the Siena Ovest exit: enter into Porta San Marco or Porta Tufi: from here you can easily reach the Duomo and leave your bike in **Via del Capitano**, just a few meters from the Piazza del Duomo.

Getting around within Siena

– **Taxi**: When your feet just can't take it anymore, in the center there are many white taxis waiting for you at several points: Piazza Indipendenza, Piazza del Duomo or Piazza Matteotti. Outside the walls at the train station (Piazzale Rosselli), at the "Le Scotte" Hospital and the Antiporto (outside Porta Camollia). You can also call the number 📞 +39 0577 49222 to have them come pick you up.

- **Si Pedala:** the City of Siena has made public bicycles available with rental stands throughout the city (both inside and outside the walls). You need to register online through **Siena Parcheggi** at 📶 www.bicincitta.com or in Via Fontebranda n. 65 (open Tuesdays and Thursdays from 9:00-12:30;15:00-16:30, 📞 +39 0577 228765).

Once you have your "card" all you have to do is touch it to the bike stand and the bike will be free for use. The first 30 minutes are always free; afterwards and for every 30 minutes following it charges a small fee. The cost for a full day is €10; for two days €15. If you prefer, you can use this service through the free App "**BicinCittà**."

Servizi

- **Public restrooms**: for men, in the city center there are still some historical urinals. Women, however, must opt for public WC's. The closest to Piazza del Campo are the following: Via di Beccheria 3, Via Casato di Sotto 14, Via di Porta Giustizia 3.

- **Luggage deposit**: in the underground area of La Lizza (Piazza Gramsci), next to the bus ticket office, from 7:00-19:00.

Palio

- **The Palio di Provenzano** is held from from June 29 - July 2, while the **Palio dell'Assunta** is from August 13-16. Don't ask the Sienese which is the most important, because all Palios are equal – as long as you win! There can also be a **Palio Straordinario**, a third Palio organized usually between May and October, for celebrating important, exceptional events.

- **The most important Palio events**: the *estrazione delle contrade* is held the last day of May in Piazza del Campo, around 7:00pm (for the July Palio), while the Sunday following the July Palio is reserved for the *estrazione* for August. One week before the day of the Palio, in the Cortile del Podestà (the courtyard in the Palazzo Pubblico) the **drappellone is presented**, the painting that will be offered up to the winning *contrada*, commissioned by the City to a local artist (July Palio) or international one (August or extraordinary Palio).

On the first of the four days of festivities (June 29 & August 13) the **tratta** takes place in Piazza del Campo, event in which the horses who will run the race are chosen through several trial runs from earlier that morning (around 8:30/9:00am). Each horse is randomly matched to one of the contrade around 1:30/2:00pm.

- **Don't miss other important events** that occur as Palio preparations begin: the **night trials** in Piazza del Campo from 5:30-7:30am, usually 1-2 days before the tratta (June 27/28 or August 11/12); the **prova generale** (the evening before the Palio) followed by dinner in all the districts; the **messa del fantino** (jockey's mass), the morning of the Palio at 7:45am in the chapel next to the Palazzo Public in Piazza del Campo; the **benedizione del cavallo** (blessing of the horse) after 2:00pm in each of the participating contrada churches.

– **Important times**: the *prove*, or trial races, occur at 9:00am and 7:45pm for the July Palio, while the August evening trials are moved up by half hour (7:15pm). The same logic is applied for the actual Palio race: on July 2 the horses enter the "track" at 7:30pm, while on August 16 at 7:00pm.

– **Where to watch the Palio**: there are two ways to see first-hand the trials and the official race. Inside the Piazza, or outside (stands/balconies/windows):
Anyone can watch the Palio in Piazza del Campo, as spots are free and standing room only. Spectators must enter the Piazza at least half hour before the beginning of the trials, as the track is then cleaned, and all exits closed off. On the day of the Palio, carefully read the section "the day of the Palio." Consider that inside the Piazza there aren't any bathrooms and, one you're in, you can't leave until the trials amd/or the Palio race have ended.

– **Spots in the stands**, on **balconies** or in **windows** are available with reserved tickets. The wooden stands on the sides of the track (**palchi**) are managed by "palcaioli," the owners of the stores and restaurants in the Piazza. Alternatively, moving up the price bracket, one can opt for a **window** or **balcony** in one of the buildings, run directly by its owners. In any case, these are **private transactions**. If you don't have Sienese friends who can do it for you, inquire at the hotel where you are staying: they certainly with have some contacts of one of these three options. Prices vary depending on the location in the Piazza, the most expensive are close to the starting point, the *mossa*. Everyone follows the rule of the "early bird catches the worm": the closer the day of the Palio, the harder it will be to find these much sought after tickets. Our advice is to act ahead to avoid risking finding spots, and certainly paying more for them.

– **The days of the Palio**: on July 2 at 16:30 the historical parade starts from the Palazzo del Governo (government building) in Piazza Duomo. It reaches and enters Piazza del Campo at 17:20, which means that around 16:40 the entrances to the Piazza begin to close, except for one: the entrance point from

Via Duprè, which remains open until 18:15. If you choose to wait until last minute (as do many Sienese), we recommend you don't wait too long to get in line, that by then will be quite long. In August everything is moved up by 30 minutes, therefore: 16:00 start of parade, entrance into Piazza at 16:50 (16:10 clearing of the track, with last entrance in Via Duprè open until 17:45).

Places of worship

- **Schedule for the masses at the cathedral:** Saturdays and Sundays at 8:00, 11:00, 12:15, 18:00 (summer 18:30). Work days: 9:30 in the Cappella Madonna del Voto. During the period when the flooring is uncovered, mass is celebrated in the **Chiesa della Santissima Annunziata**, in front of the cathedral.
- The **Synagogue** and **Jewish Museum** are in Vicolo delle Scotte 14: religious ceremonies on Saturdays and in occasion of Jewish holidays. Open to the public between October 1 and May 31 on Sundays, Mondays and Thursdays from 10:30-17:30. From June 1 - September 30 on Sundays and Mondays from 11-18 and Tuesdays, Wednesdays and Thursdays from 14-18. +39 0577 286300, www.jewishtuscany.it.

Art and Shows

- Santa Maria della Scala Museum: Piazza del Duomo 2, +39 0577 228744, www.santamariadellascala.com. From March 15 – October 15, open from 10:00-19:00 (Thursdays until 22:00).
From October 16-March 14, during the week open from 10:00-17:00, closed on Tuesdays. Saturdays and Sundays from 10:00-19:00.

- **Duomo Museum**: www.operaduomo.siena.it/visita. To visit the entire museum complex there is an all-inclusive ticket called the **Opa Si Pass**, that includes the Cathedral, Baptistery, Crypt, Duomo Museum, Facciatone, Oratorio di San Bernardino and the Diocese Museum of Holy Art. The ticket is valid for three days (consecutive) and the price varies according to season (13€/15€). For information and reservations: +39 0577 286300.
The Gate of Heaven ticket gives visitors access to the Duomo's rooftop (cost is €22), with guided tours beginning every half hour, following the cathedral's opening hours.

- **Museo Civico**: Siena's Civic Museum, Piazza del Campo 1 (entrance in the Cortile del Podestà, in the courtyard of the Palazzo Pubblico): open every day from 10:00-18:00 in the winter months (ticket office closes at 17:15). During the rest of the year the museum closes at 19:00. Closed on Christmas Day; on New Year's Day open from

12:00-18:00. Tickets are available online at ⟨⟩ www.comune.siena.it (9-10€).
For more info: ✉ ticket@comune. siena.it, ☎ +39 0577 2926 14 / 292615.

- **Torre del Mangia** - Piazza del Campo 1: between November 1-February 28 open every day from 10:00-16:00 (ticket office closes at 15:15. From March 1-October 31, open until 19:00 (ticket office closes at 18:15). The tower may be closed for safety reasons because of bad weather. It is also closed on Christmas Day; on New Year's Day open from 12:00-16:00. Tickets are €10, and there are discounts for family groups. ☎ +39 0577 292614 / 292615.

- **Pinacoteca Nazionale** - Via San Pietro 29: public museum open Tuesdays - Saturdays 9:00-19:00, Sundays, Mondays and holidays from 9:00-13:30 (ticket office open until 30 minutes before closing time). The opening hours may be reduced for certain holidays.
Tickets: €6, €2 for special discounts. Free entrance the first Sunday of every month for #**Domenicalmuseo** (#Sundaysatthemuseum) (⟨⟩ www. pinacotecanazionale.siena.it).

- **Museo San Donato** (Monte dei Paschi di Siena bank) - Piazza Salimbeni 3: part of the complex of buildings part of the Monte dei Paschi di Siena bank, the famous **Rocca Salimbeni**, which also houses the historical archives of the bank. The San Donato Museum (originally a church) is a true treasure full of works of art. It is open and free to the public on the mornings of July 2 and August 15 and the first Saturday of October (in occasion of the "Invito a Palazzo" initiative, inviting the public to this museum, promoted by ABI, the Italian Banking Association). For information and reservations, ⟨⟩ www.mpsart.it.

- **Museo dell'Acqua** - Water Museum, Strada delle Fonti di Pescaia 1 (⟨⟩www.museoacqua.comune. siena.it). Open by reservation only from Monday-Friday 9:00-13:30 (☎ +39 0577 292614-5) or by email ✉ ticket@comune.siena. it indicating date, number of participants and phone number. The same procedure is valid for planning visits to the **Bottini di Fonte Gaia** or **Fonte Nuova**. For these visits it's necessary to come "armed" with flashlight and proper shoes (or boots). This visit is not recommended for children under 8 years old or anyone who suffers from claustrophobia.

- **Fondazione Accademia Musicale Chigiana** - Chigiana Music Academy, via di Città 89: the Academy is located inside the beautiful Palazzo Chigi Saracini, other than works of art, books and antique musical instruments, boasts an intense year-round concert program at the international level (🔊 www.chigiana.org). To reserve a guided visit to the Palazzo contact: ✉ visite@chigiana.it or by phone at 📞 +39 0577 22091 (Monday-Friday, 9:00 - 13:00).

- **Archivio di Stato** - State Archives, via Banchi di Sotto 52: the Biccherne Museum and its Archives are open to visitors Monday-Saturday at 10:00, 11:00, 12:00 (and closes at 13:00). It is closed on national and local holidays. 📞 +39 0577 247145, 🔊 www.archiviodistato.siena.it.

- **Theaters**: the theatrical season for the City of Siena (🔊 www.comune.siena.it) takes place in two different theaters: the **Teatro dei Rozzi** in Piazza Indipendenza 15 and **Teatro dei Rinnovati** in Piazza del Campo 1. Online reservations at: 🔊 www.teatridisiena.it, ✉ teatrisiena@comune.siena.it.

- **Siena Jazz**: the Accademia Nazionale del Jazz (National Jazz Academy) is located inside the Fortress (Piazza Caduti delle Forze Armate) at number 10. 📞 +39 0577 271401, 🔊 www.sienajazz.it.

Free time
- **What to pack**: comfortable walking shoes are essential. The city is a continuous up and down, and the cobblestones put feet and ankles to the test. For smart packing here is an idea of average monthly temperatures: January (1-10°C, 34-50°F), February (3-12°C, 37-54°F), March (5-15°C, 41-59°F), April (8-19°C, 46-66°F), May (11-23°C, 52-73°F), June (15-27°C, 59-81°F), July (17-31°C, 63-88°F), August (17-31°C, 63-88°F), September (14-27°C, 57-81°F), October (10-21°C, 50-70°F), November (6-15°C, 43-59°F), December (2-10°C, 36-50°F).

- **Where to stay**: There is a variety of choices per price range: from hostels (Siena Hostel Guidoriccio) to numerous B&Bs. If you're looking for a chicer option, look for residenze d'epoca (historical residences) or villas in the countryside. For hotels in the city, there are all sizes and shapes, but the only 5-star hotel within the historical center is the Grand Hotel Continental.

- **Picnic areas**: inside the walls, the ideal place for a packed lunch is in Piazza del Mercato, under the **Tartarugone** (big turtle shell), a 19th century covered pavilion in the middle of the piazza, where you can enjoy its open space and beautiful view: a true "balcony" overlooking the countryside. Outside of the city, convenient for who has a car, can stop at the city park in Strada di Pescaia: called the **Parco Unità d'Italia**, it has a cycling track, outdoor gym equipment, play area for children and even a gated dog park. You can eat at the picnic tables, drink from the water fountain and even grill out on one of the four barbecues.

- **Siena for kids**: even the littlest tourists are welcome in town. There are various attractions, starting from the **Interactive Museum** in the Santa Maria della Scala, where games and experimentation are possible. There are also numerous parks: the two main ones are the **Giardini della Lizza**, next to Piazza Gramsci, a traditional meeting point for Sienese children and the **Parco delle Rimembranze**, behind the fortress, with a splendid marble barberi track where children can recreate the lively pace of the Palio. Don't forget the **Giardino dei profumi**, in the Piazzetta Marco Cioni inside Porta Pispini and the **Parco di Piazza Amendola** with slides, playground and a large field area where you can even play quidditch, the famous game from Harry Potter.

- **Cooking lessons**: courses organized year round at the **Scuola di cucina di Lella**, in Via Fontebranda 69 www.scuoladicucinadilella.net, the **Scuola di Cucina Fonte Giusta**, in via Camollia 102, www.scuoladicucinafontegiusta.com, and the **Scuola di Cucina International Chef Academy**,

right outside the walls, in Viale Europa 1, www.internationalchefacademy.com.

- **Hot springs** (with resort-style spas) are in the areas surrounding Siena: in Rapolano Terme, Terme Antica Querciolaia (+39 0577 724091) and Terme di San Giovanni (+39 0577 724039). In Monticiano, Terme Bagni di Petriolo (+39 0577 757104). In the Val d'Orcia, Terme Bagno Vignoni (+39 0577 887150) and Terme San Filippo (+39 0577 872982). In Chianciano, Terme di Chianciano (+39 0578 68501) and Terme di Sant'Elena (+39 0578 321728). We also recommend the Terme Fonteverde di San Casciano dei Bagni (+39 0578 57241) and Terme di Montepulciano (+39 0578 791207).

- **Swimming Pools**: the public swimming pool in Piazza Amendola is indoor (+39 0577 47496), while Acquacalda has both indoor and outdoor options (+39 0577 52667).

- **Shopping**: Via Banchi di Sopra e Via Banchi di Sotto, Via di Città, Via dei Montanini and Via di Pantaneto: these streets are the heart of shopping in Siena. Indulge in the historical shops (such as Cortecci, since 1935), recent boutiques, international brands (Benetton, Liu Jo, Max&Co., Twin-set, Falconeri,

Dixie, Stefanel, Boggi, Intimissimi, Sephora, etc.) or local run stores (Franchi, Falchini, Cappelleria Terzi). For those nostalgic for artisan shops, there are numerous print shops, tapestry and furniture stores, as well as other vintage shops.

- **Malls and shopping centers**: the three main ones are the Porta Siena in front of the train station and the commercial centers in Viale Toselli and Strada Massetana Romana. Inside the walls, there is a small commercial complex called the Galleria Metropolitan (with its own cinema, large terrace and view of the Duomo).

- **Markets**: Wednesday is the day of the **weekly market** at the **Lizza** (8:00-13:00 approx.), that fills the streets around the Fortress. An **antique market** takes place in Piazza del Mercato the third Sunday of every month, under the Tartarugone pavilion. The **"Mercato nel Campo"** is a must-see, held in Piazza del Campo the first weekend of December (sometimes an additional edition in the Spring). **Siena in Fiore** (Siena in Flower) instead fills the adjacent gardens to the fountain of San Prospero, along the walls of the Fortress: it is a market/show for plants, flowers and garden accessories, open to the public, usually held during a weekend between May and October (🔊 www.societatoscanaorticultura.it).

Other city festivities: **Santa Lucia** (Saint Lucy day: December 13) and **San Giuseppe** (St. Joseph day, also Father's Day in Italy: March 19).

- **For your photographs**, here are some of the best views and landscapes:
1. From the top of the **Facciatone**, entrance from the Museo Opera della Metropolitana: a 360° panorama of Siena at your feet and the countryside on the horizon.
2. On the **Costarella dei Barbieri**: the photo that every tourist takes to capture the entire shell of Piazza del Campo.
3. Entering Piazza del Campo from **Chiasso del Bargello** or even **Via Rinaldini** you can admire the full height of the Torre del Mangia, with a beautiful chiaroscuro contrast in the background.
4. Another great angle for admiring the Tower: at the top of Via Duprè, when **Via Sant'Agata** begins, turn around. The Arch of San Giuseppe (next to the Church) is a natural frame of the sloping street, that seems to close in around the merlons of the Palazzo Pubblico and the Tower.
5. From the steps of the **Basilica di Santa Maria dei Servi**, at sundown, the city offers a splendid silhouette on the bell tower of the cathedral and the Tower.
6. From **Via Diacceto**, a wonderful view of the Basilica of San Domenico and on the steep Via Fontebranda hill.

7. From the top of the bastions of the **Fortezza Medicea** (Fortress) you seem to "dominate" the city center. The last lights of the day paint orange stripes on the Tower and the Duomo.
8. From **Via Camporegio**, going down from the Basilica of San Domenico; on the right it seems to almost touch the cathedral, while to the left the point of the Tower can be seen over the rooftops.
9. Immersed in the green space of the **Orto de' Pecci**, or from the top of the **Orto dei Tolomei,** you can enjoy an unprecedented view of the Palazzo Pubblico and of its loggia from behind.

– **If the city center** isn't enough for you, the **Sienese countryside** is famous for its variety and its beauty. There are five must-visit areas, all UNESCO heritage sites: the **Val di Merse, Crete Senesi, Monte Amiata, Val d'Orcia** and **Chianti** to the south, while **Val d'Elsa, San Gimignano** and **Montagnola** to the north, without forgetting the fortress town of **Monteriggioni** with its beautifully preserved medieval atmosphere, so close to the gates of Siena.

– **Moving southeast** by car to the countryside, the **Crete Senesi** are an area not to miss. In twenty minutes, taking the Siena-Bettolle highway, take the Taverne d'Arbia exit and follow the directions for Asciano.

Along the privincial street 438, turn to look once you've reached the top of the hill, near **Vescona**: from there you can "capture" Siena immersed in these famous crete, with the typical grey tones on the **Strada di Leonina**, almost colorless, reminiscent of the lunar surface.

– **The cypress forest**: one of the most famous postcard landscapes of Tuscany. On the Strada regionale 2, between **Torrenieri** and **San Quirico d'Orcia**, you'll surely run into cars stopped on the side of the road taking pictures. From the Via Cassia you can see a rhombus-shaped dense forest, a wonderful sight in all seasons. But don't stop there: there is another one, on the white adjacent street, that you can access from the hidden Strada di Riguardo. It's the "circle of cypresses," where the trees form two unexpected semicircles right in the middle of the street.

– **The Strada Provinciale 88** is very photogenic, with is uphill slope and its cypresses, toward **Monticchiello**. The best point of observation is from the parallel and surrounding white streets. Adventure out and get lost: the search for the best shot is well worth it as the Val d'Orcia is truly a unique vision.

– **Nearby**, this time between Pienza and San Quirico d'Orcia, another view worth immortalizing is the **Cappella della Madonna di Vitaleta**. Many artists have been inspired by this little late-Renaissance church immersed in cypresses and vineyards, giving it its timeless charm.

ALL THINGS CHANGE...

The information provided in this book was personally verified by the authors and updated in March 2023. As we know, the world changes at lightning speed: we recommend that these indications are used as general guidelines that should be double-checked before making plans, just so you don't find yourselves unprepared. If you notice any discrepancies, help us out by notifying us for future editions: ✉ info@morellinieditore.it

Index of Streets and Places of Interest

HEARTFELT THANKS

If along our ten paths we never felt alone, it is due to the affection of friends and experts who showered us with advice and direction.

Thank you to: Christina Angelilli, Duccio Balestracci, Debora Barbagli, Massimo Biliorsi, Chiara Bratto, Giulia Brogi, Marilena Caciorgna, Elena Casi, Andrea Ceccherini, Mattia Cella, Lella Ciampoli, Martina Dei, Roberto Faleri, Katiuscia Girolami, Enrico Grassini, Stefano Jacoviello, Paolo Lazzeroni, Andrea Lensini, Luca Leoni, Luciano Livi, Barbara Lusini, Mike Manchester, Roberta Mari, Annalisa Marraccini, Maura Martellucci, Michele Occhioni, Sonia Pallai, Giovanni Pellicci, Lucia Pelosi, Claudio Taccioli, Antonio Tasso, Luciano Valentini, Carlo Vigni.

A special thank you to: Associazione Centro Guide Siena, Associazione Le Mura, Comune di Siena, Consorzio per la Tutela del Palio di Siena, Federagit Siena, SIS Intercultural Study Abroad.